GUIDED
INSTRUCTION

DOUGLAS | NANCY
FISHER | FREY

GUIDED
INSTRUCTION

How to Develop
Confident and
Successful Learners

1703 N. Beauregard St. • Alexandria, VA 22311-1714 USA
Phone: 800-933-2723 or 703-578-9600 • Fax: 703-575-5400
Web site: www.ascd.org • E-mail: member@ascd.org
Author guidelines: www.ascd.org/write

Gene R. Carter, *Executive Director;* Judy Zimny, *Chief Program Development Officer;* Nancy Modrak, *Publisher;* Scott Willis, *Director, Book Acquisitions & Development;* Julie Houtz, *Director, Book Editing & Production;* Leah Lakins, *Editor;* Reece Quiñones, *Senior Graphic Designer;* Mike Kalyan, *Production Manager;* Valerie Younkin, *Typesetter;* Carmen Yuhas, *Production Specialist*

Printed in the United States of America. Cover art © 2010 by ASCD. ASCD publications present a variety of viewpoints. The views expressed or implied in this book should not be interpreted as official positions of the Association.

PAPERBACK ISBN: 978-1-4166-1068-7   ASCD product # 111017   n10/10

Also available as an e-book (see Books in Print for the ISBNs).

Quantity discounts for the paperback edition only: 10–49 copies, 10%; 50+ copies, 15%; for 1,000 or more copies, call 800-933-2723, ext. 5634, or 703-575-5634. For desk copies: member@ascd.org.

Library of Congress Cataloging-in-Publication Data
Fisher, Douglas, 1965–
    Guided instruction : how to develop confident and successful learners / Douglas Fisher and Nancy Frey.
        p. cm.
    Includes bibliographical references and index.
    ISBN 978-1-4166-1068-7 (pbk. : alk. paper)   1. Teachers—United States   2. Teaching—United States—Psychological aspects.   3. Teacher-student relationships—United States.   4. Motivation in education—United States.   5. Learning, Psychology of. I. Frey, Nancy, 1959- II. Title.
    LB1775.2.F596 2010
    371.39—dc22

20 19 18 17 16 15 14 13 12 11 10   1 2 3 4 5 6 7 8 9 10 11 12

GUIDED INSTRUCTION

How to Develop Confident and Successful Learners

Introduction

As teachers, we are at our best when we guide learners to new or deeper understandings. We feel that sense of pride when the learner grasps a new concept, whether it's breaking the code in learning to read or explaining how a calculus problem was solved. Regardless of the grade or subject we teach, our role as educators revolves around the idea that we guide learning.

We chose the word *guide* intentionally because it means to steer or direct a course. It's showing the way for the learner, but not doing it. In popular educational terminology, it's scaffolding. In essence, *guided instruction is saying or doing the just-right thing to get the learner to do cognitive work.*

We've all experienced this kind of instruction. Nancy remembers her statistics class in graduate school. Already threatened by the subject matter, she wasn't sure that she could pass the class. Looking to the assigned text for the course was no help because it assumed extensive prior knowledge and was written in technical language. Thankfully, Nancy had a teacher who understood the need to transfer responsibility to the learners through intentional teacher moves. For example, during a discussion early in the semester that stands out in Nancy's mind, the teacher started with a question to check for understanding:

"What are the main differences between qualitative and quantitative research?" When the students did not answer, the teacher did not get mad. The teacher did not yell or blame the students. The teacher did not start calling on students at random to show that they either hadn't read or didn't understand what they had been assigned to read. And most important, she did not simply tell them the answer.

Unfortunately, some students are not guided, they're told. And telling doesn't result in learning. Although there is a role for direct explanation and modeling, which we discuss later in this book, telling students things over and over (and perhaps more slowly and more loudly) does not result in their understanding. Students need to be guided to understanding; they deserve nothing less from their teachers.

So what did Nancy's teacher do? The teacher used a combination of questions, prompts, cues, direct explanations, and modeling to guide students' learning. Having already questioned the group, the teacher added prompts and cues such as these:

- "One of the words has *quantify* as its root. That should help."
- "Some people say that it's 'soft' research, but there are still specific procedures used to collect data."
- "Remember the study we examined on dropouts that had all of the outcome data. That was quantitative."

Through the teacher's intentional moves, Nancy learned the content. And that's what guided instruction is all about—ensuring that the learner (and not just the teacher) engages in cognitive work.

Guided instruction, although critical, is not sufficient to ensure lasting understanding. Students also need to experience expert modeling, engage in productive tasks with their peers, and produce individual work. In other words, guided instruction is part of a bigger instructional picture in which students consolidate and apply their learning.

Guided Instruction in the Bigger Instructional Picture

This book is a natural outgrowth of our work on the gradual release of responsibility, outlined in our book *Better Learning Through Structured Teaching* (Fisher & Frey, 2008). First proposed in 1983 (Pearson & Gallagher), the Gradual Release of Responsibility model of instruction suggests that cognitive work should shift slowly and intentionally from teacher-as-model, to joint responsibility between teacher and student, to independent practice and application by the learner. The Gradual Release of Responsibility model provides a structure for the teacher to move from assuming "all the responsibility for performing a task ... to a situation in which the students assume all of the responsibility" (Duke & Pearson, 2002, p. 211). Over time, students assume more responsibility for the task, moving from being participants in the modeled lessons, to apprentices in guided instruction, to collaborators with their peers, and finally, to independent performers (see Figure I.1).

The Gradual Release of Responsibility model is built on several theories, including the following:

- Piaget's (1952) work on cognitive structures and schema
- Vygotsky's (1962, 1978) work on zones of proximal development
- Bandura's (1965, 1977) work on attention, retention, reproduction, and motivation
- Wood, Bruner, and Ross's (1976) work on scaffolded instruction

Taken together, these theories suggest that learning occurs through interactions with others, and when these interactions are intentional, specific learning occurs.

Our framework for implementing the gradual release of responsibility includes the following components:

- *Focus lessons*—Teachers establish the lesson's purpose and model their own thinking to illustrate for students how to approach the new learning.
- *Guided instruction*—Teachers strategically use questions and assessment-informed prompts, cues, direct explanations, and modeling to guide students

to increasingly complex thinking and facilitate students' increased responsibility for task completion.

• *Productive group work*—Teachers design and supervise tasks that enable students to consolidate their thinking and understanding—and that require students to generate individual products that can provide formative assessment information.

• *Independent tasks*—Teachers design and supervise tasks that require students to apply information they have been taught to create new and authentic products. This phase of the instructional framework is ideal for the "spiral review" that so many educators know their students need, and it is a way to build students' confidence by allowing them to demonstrate their expanding competence.

Figure I.1 | **A Structure for Instruction**

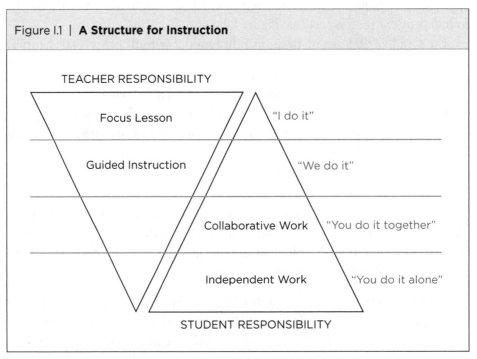

Source: From *Better Learning Through Structured Teaching* (p. 4), by D. Fisher and N. Frey, 2008, Alexandria, VA: ASCD.

Our focus in this book is on guided instruction, which can be done with the whole class, small groups, or individual students. Guided instruction is not a classroom structure or routine, but rather a set of teacher behaviors that ensure student learning. Having said that, it is important to note that needs-based small-group instruction is one of the more effective tools we teachers have to facilitate student learning. In fact, we would go so far as to say that the absence of small-group guided instruction that is based on student needs as determined by formative assessment places students at risk for school failure.

We like to think of guided instruction as the moves of an expert teacher, because saying the just-right thing is hard to plan in advance. Guided instruction requires knowledge of the learner and the expectations for thinking at a given grade or age level. That's not to say that there aren't guided instruction materials available for sale; there are. But it's really teacher expertise that matters, as the teacher has to know when to use questions, prompts, cues, direct explanations, or modeling to get the learner to learn. Let's take a look inside a classroom to see how this framework might play out.

Productive Group Work and Independent Tasks During Guided Instruction

Developing student competence requires a number of strategic moves by the teacher, especially if students are expected to remember and use the information later in life. We're often asked what the other students are doing while the teacher provides guided instruction. Our answer involves both productive group work and independent tasks (Frey, Fisher, & Everlove, 2009).

Productive group work requires that students talk with each other, interacting with the content and the language of the lesson. Students should be expected to use the vocabulary that has been taught as they work to complete various tasks. But they should also each be held accountable for individual contributions. In fact, that accountability is the key to productive group work. Students have to interact with one another *and* they have to each produce something that the teacher can use to determine understanding and next steps of instruction.

Independent tasks are also an important component of classroom instruction. These tasks range from independent reading to formative and summative assessments. Ideally, independent tasks are an application of what students have learned in class. These tasks should not be piles of worksheets, rote memorization, or necessarily silent and solitary. Instead, independent learning tasks should have the following characteristics:

- Be based on meaningful learning activities
- Enable individual learners to take responsibility for their own learning
- Be essential for lifelong motivation and growth
- Prepare students for their role as responsible citizens in a changing society

Of course, in any given classroom, some students might be engaged in productive group work tasks while some of their peers are completing independent tasks, and still others are meeting with the teacher for guided instruction. In other classrooms, all of the students may be engaged in productive group work, with the teacher meeting with smaller groups to extend their understanding through guided instruction. Remember, guided instruction is a teacher behavior, not a classroom structure. Teachers can structure their classrooms in a number of different ways to ensure that students receive guided instruction.

Let's look at an example. After establishing the purpose of the lesson, Mr. Martinez models his thinking while editing a paper he wrote the day before. He uses a laptop and an interactive whiteboard so that students can observe his composing process and listen to his thinking while he writes. In this particular lesson, Mr. Martinez is thinking about his sentence leads, the first three or four words that start each sentence. Using the yellow-highlight function, Mr. Martinez highlights the first three words of each sentence in his introductory paragraph. He reads just the highlighted words aloud and then says, "Wow, I really like what I've said here. I don't use the same phrases to start my sentences. I think that this helps the reader pay attention to the points I'm raising. I also noticed that my sentences are all on the same topic, so that paragraph hangs together well. I remember that I used the introduction technique of startling statistic, and I'm still thinking that it works for my topic to kind of shock my readers with something that makes them pay attention. Now I'll take a look at my second paragraph."

With his formatting palette and yellow-highlight function, Mr. Martinez returns to his paper and highlights the first three words of each sentence in the second paragraph. When he finishes, several students whisper and point. One of them says under her breath, "Too many of the same starts. Not great." Mr. Martinez reads just the highlighted words aloud and, when he finishes, he says, "I even made myself bored. I'm saying the same thing three different times. And if I'm bored, I can't imagine what my reader is thinking. I have to fix this. I have a responsibility to my readers to keep them interested in my topic. I know that sometimes I can use the same sentence starts for effect, like the persuasive technique of repetition or the way some poets do, but the words in my paragraph are not really worthy of being repeated. Can I get some help? Could you four make several recommendations for the first sentence? And can you five make several recommendations here, where I repeated it?"

Mr. Martinez asks groups of students to talk about what he has written and then make several recommendations for revision of his sentences. They write their recommendations out on chart paper, each student using a different-colored marker. Mr. Martinez knows that this added individual account-ability—making their contributions recognizable by color—ensures that all students participate in the task.

When the groups have completed the task, Mr. Martinez asks for their attention and reviews what they have written. He says, "I know that, as the writer, I can choose which suggestions I want to use and which I don't want to use. I see that there are 14 different suggestions for this first sentence. Let's try something. Let's each vote on which one we like best, and we'll see if there is a favorite. Do you have your clickers ready? Go."

At this point, each student enters the number of a preferred revision, and after a few seconds, Mr. Martinez has the computer graph the results. There is no clear winner, and Mr. Martinez says, "Interesting. You all seem to like different revisions, and that's the power of getting advice from readers. There are lots and lots of ideas to choose from. I think I'll choose number four and make that change here."

Mr. Martinez continues this process for the next few minutes and revises his paragraph along the way. When he is done, he reminds students that as they edit their own papers, they need to provide each other with lots of ideas so that the writer can choose one to use. The students then move into their groups and begin working. The groups represent the academic diversity in the classroom, and Mr. Martinez has a reason for each student's being in each group. (More on grouping students can be found in the final chapter of this book.)

Each student individually highlights the first three words of each sentence using a colored highlighter pen. One student reads the highlighted words from his paper aloud at a time, pausing at each paragraph for the others in the group to talk about the repetitious phrases. Each member of the group then adds recommendations to the chart paper using the assigned color markers, and the author of the paper incorporates this feedback into a new draft. This process continues as each member of the group receives peer feedback.

But some of the students in Mr. Martinez's room haven't finished their first complete draft and thus are not ready for peer feedback and editing. These students work independently at this time, completing their papers. During this time, Mr. Martinez meets with groups of students, using guided instruction to further their understanding. As he calls students to meet with him at a table, they leave their productive group work tasks.

The first group Mr. Martinez meets with consists of three students who regularly make mechanical mistakes while writing, so Mr. Martinez wants to address this need. He asks each student to check for capitalization and ending punctuation for each sentence. He reminds them that they are to put their finger on the capital letter and then follow that to the ending punctuation. Of course, Mr. Martinez knows that there might be run-on sentences, fragments, and other errors, but he wants to check to see if this group can identify the beginnings and endings of their sentences. When Mariah misses one, Mr. Martinez says, "Look again at the sentence that starts with *When.*" Mariah does so, but doesn't seem to get the point. Mr. Martinez says, "Follow that sentence to its end." Mariah does so correctly and notices that there is no ending punctuation before the next capitalized letter. Correcting this, Mariah continues reading her paper. Mr. Martinez turns his attention to Joseph and says, "Be on the lookout for words in the middle of the sentence that should be capitalized. You don't want ending punctuation there, right, Joseph?" Joseph rereads the section of his paper and notices that he has added a period before the word *Saturday*, which is in the middle of the sentence. As they finish reading for capitalization and punctuation errors, Mr. Martinez turns their attention to spelling by saying, "Remember, if the words are on our wall, they should always be spelled correctly in our papers. They're the no-excuse words. Let's reread to make sure all of the no-excuse words are correct." The students begin this process with Mr. Martinez prompting and cueing along the way. After 20 minutes, these students return to their groups, and Mr. Martinez calls another group.

Five students join him at the table. Each member of this group writes very well—which illustrates, in part, why guided instruction with small groups matters so much. While students complete tasks with their peers in mixed-ability groups, the teacher can select specific students to guide into deeper understanding. Mr. Martinez tell this group that they'll be looking at word choice and making sure that they are using words that have a "razzle-dazzle" effect on the reader. He says, "Of course, we have to use the words correctly. But we need to think about exchanging everyday words for words that wow and impress the reader. We don't want to go overboard with this, but we do want to show that we have a good command of vocabulary and that we can choose the just-right word for the situation. So I thought we'd use this time for you to reflect on your papers and consider alternative word choices. Of course, I'll be talking with you as you do so." The students begin, as they have before, by reading with a blue pen in hand, circling words that they might want to replace. As Khadijah circles the word *walked*, Mr. Martinez asks her what she sees in her mind at that point in the text. Khadijah says, "Well, it's not really just walking. It's more like slow and moving side to side. I'm thinking that there's a better word for that, but I'll have to find it."

Satisfied that she's on her way, Mr. Martinez turns his attention to James, who hasn't yet identified any words. Mr. Martinez says, "You like what you've written, right?" James says yes. Mr. Martinez says, "You know that it's OK to consider words to change but not change them if the choices aren't any better. Maybe you could just show me that there are a few words you could change—like in that second sentence of the second paragraph. Anything come to mind?" James rereads the sentence and circles *said* and *happy*. Turning to Mr. Martinez, James agrees that there are words that could be changed. "I guess these words work, but they're kind of tired. I mean that everyone says them all the time. I didn't really notice before. I might change out those words to make a point. You know, to add that punch."

This is what guided instruction is all about: teachers scaffold students' understanding. It's taking students from where they are to where they can be. It's about closing the achievement gap and raising expectations through intentional instruction. As we have said before, it's saying or doing the just-right thing to get the learner to engage in cognitive work.

A Categorical System for Guided Instruction

In this book, we provide a categorical system for implementing guided instruction. Of course, guided instruction has to be part of an overall instructional framework, as we have described. Our system for guided instruction has four parts:

- *Questioning* to check for understanding
- *Prompting* to facilitate students' cognitive and metacognitive processes and processing
- *Cueing* to shift students' attention to focus on specific information, errors, or partial understandings
- *Explaining and modeling* when students do not have sufficient knowledge to complete tasks

Our categorical system is based on our own teaching, observations of hundreds and hundreds of teachers who have invited us into their classrooms to observe experts at work, and reviews of the published research on quality teaching. Interestingly, the terms we use are commonly used interchangeably or confused with one another. For example, someone might say *verbal prompt* and another person might say *verbal cue*. Similarly, someone might say *cue* and *prompt* as if they are synonyms. We've tried to clarify the similarities and differences among these terms to help teachers implement quality teaching for all students. But we don't want to get bogged down in semantic debates about specific terms. It's the *intent*—the teacher's intent—in using the question, prompt, cue, explanation, or model that we're most interested in. We hope you are interested as well and that you find this book helpful as you guide learners to deep understanding of the ever-changing world around them.

Scaffolds for Learning:
The Key to Guided Instruction

The underlying idea for learning scaffolds is relatively old. Most people trace the concept to Lev Vygotsky's (1978) idea of the "zone of proximal development." Vygotsky believed that a learner's developmental level consisted of two parts: the "actual developmental level" and the "potential developmental level." The zone of proximal development, then, is "the distance between the actual developmental level as determined by independent problem solving and the level of potential development as determined through problem solving under adult guidance, or in collaboration with more capable peers" (p. 86). In Vygotsky's words, the zone of proximal development "awakens a variety of internal developmental processes that are able to operate only when the child is interacting with people in his environment" (p. 90).

The zone of proximal development can also be described as the difference between what a learner can do independently and what can be accomplished with the help of a "more knowledgeable other." This concept is critical for understanding how to scaffold learning. The more knowledgeable other, who can be an adult or a peer, shares knowledge with the learner to bridge the gap between what is known and what is not known. When the learner has expanded her knowledge, the actual developmental level has been increased and the zone of proximal development has shifted upward. In other words, the zone of proximal development is ever changing as the learner validates and extends knowledge. This process is what led Vygotsky to write: "Through others, we become ourselves" (Rieber, 1998, p. 170).

But Vygotsky did not use the term *scaffold* or *scaffolding*. The term *scaffold*, as applied to learning situations, comes from Wood, Bruner, and Ross (1976), who define it as a process "that enables a child or novice to solve a task or achieve a goal that would be beyond his unassisted efforts" (p. 90). As they note, scaffolds require the adult's "controlling those elements of the task that are initially beyond the learner's capability, thus permitting him to concentrate upon and complete only those elements that are within his range of competence" (p. 90). For example, in teaching a child to ride a bike, the training wheels serve as one scaffold. The adult running alongside the bike serves as another. In other words, the adult handles the harder parts temporarily, while allowing the child to try out the easier parts.

Like scaffolds that hold a building in place as it's constructed, "scaffolding is actually a bridge used to build upon what students already know to arrive at something they do not know. If scaffolding is properly administered, it will act as an enabler, not as a disabler" (Benson, 1997, p. 126). According to Greenfield (1999),

> The scaffold, as it is known in building construction, has five characteristics: it provides a support; it functions as a tool; it extends the range of the worker; it allows a worker to accomplish a task not otherwise possible; and it is used to selectively aid the worker where needed. (p. 118)

Dixon, Carnine, and Kameenui (1993) remind us that effective scaffolds must be "gradually dismantled" in order to remain effective (p. 100). However, if scaffolds are dismantled too quickly, learning does not occur and the learner becomes frustrated in the process.

You probably have noticed that we use the term *scaffold* as a noun rather than a verb, because a present-tense verb may imply a process that is ongoing, which places teachers and students at risk of dependency rather than independence.

What's Going On in the Brain?

All of the theorists and researchers we have focused on thus far have one important thing in common: they're trying to influence what's inside the learner's brain. That's what teachers are trying to do as well. Teachers really are brain workers. We're not suggesting that the neurosciences have all of the answers that we need to effectively teach. We acknowledge the concerns about relying too heavily on brain science (Bruer, 1997). For example, Willingham (2008) says, "I don't understand what my computer hardware is doing as I type this reply, but if I did, that knowledge would not change how I typed or what I wrote" (p. 422). But we think Willingham understands something more important about his computer hard drive—namely, the best ways to store and retrieve information. And that's our goal here. As teachers, we have to be aware of the best ways to help students store and retrieve information.

We know that worksheets aren't going to do it. As has been said before, "worksheets don't grow dendrites" (Tate, 2003). We also know that simply telling students something isn't going to do it. After all, how many times have you remembered everything you heard? Thankfully, there are things we can do to ensure that students learn. At the most basic level, we have to get those things into students' working memory and then have them use those things so that they move to long-term memory.

Larry Squire, a professor of psychiatry and neuroscience, and Eric Kandel, a neurobiologist and Nobel prize winner in medicine, demonstrated that there are three areas of the brain involved in the early stages of learning a new skill or procedure: the prefrontal cortex, the parietal cortex, and the cerebellum. These three areas allow the learner to pay attention, to execute the correct movements, and to sequence steps. Squire and Kandel's (2000) research, and the research of others that they summarize, suggest that as a task or procedure is learned, these three brain areas become *less* involved as the sensory-motor cortex takes over. In other words, more cognitive "space" is devoted to learning a new skill than executing a learned skill. This is one place where instructional scaffolds help. The teacher can provide temporary support for students as they use more space to learn something and remove that support when they have learned it.

Hebb (1949), a psychologist who significantly influenced the field of neuropsychology, suggests that as neuronal pathways are used repeatedly, they begin to change physically and form steadily faster networks. Hebb's principle, "neurons that fire together, wire together," is echoed in the theory of automaticity (LaBerge & Samuels, 1974). As these pathways are used with ever-increasing efficiency, the skills become more automatic, creating the necessary "think time" to form new connections. In other words, as specific tasks become automatic, working memory is available for meaning making.

Automaticity is dependent on a learner's working memory. Despite attempts to cram lots of information into a brain all at once, neuroscience research confirms Miller's (1956) finding that humans can work with about seven new and previously unassociated bits of information at a time. Interestingly, this limitation is removed when information from long-term memory is moved back into working memory to complete a task (Ericsson & Kintsch, 1995). Again, this finding has important implications for teacher behaviors. We have to provide students scaffolds when they are working with new or previously unassociated information, but we do not need to provide scaffolds when students are working with known information.

Teachers need to chunk information in ways that are consistent with working memory and long-term transfer. One of the ways to do this is through work with schemas, or mental structures that represent content. Tools such as concept maps, word webs, and graphic organizers provide students with schemas that they can use to organize information (Guthrie, Wigfield, & Barbosa, 2004). These are scaffolds—temporary supports—that provide students with organizational systems for learning content.

But even more than that, an understanding of memory systems has profound implications for instruction, which include creating systematic and intentional scaffolds of students' understanding rather than leaving them alone to discover information independently. That's not to say that students should not work together in collaborative learning; they should. We have argued for productive group work in which students interact with one another and generate ideas to produce individual works (Frey et al., 2009). But this work must center on the consolidation and application of content that students already know. It's neither the time nor the place to introduce new information. Doing so would overload the working memory system and fail to ensure learning.

Although we advocate productive group work, we do not argue for turning classrooms into places devoid of guidance from the teacher. Our experience and reviews of the research suggest that the teacher must be involved in guided instruction, using appropriate scaffolds, while students are engaged in productive group work with their peers. Scaffolds reduce the demand on working memory. As Kirschner, Sweller, and Clark (2006) note, we cannot "proceed with no reference to the characteristics of working memory, long-term memory, or the intricate relations between them" (p. 76). That does not mean that we rely only on direct instruction and simply telling students what they need to know. Rather, we need to guide students to new levels of understanding and ensure that they have a wealth of opportunities to practice and use that information so that it moves into long-term memory and can then be accessed by working memory without the constraints of the number of items that can be used (Sweller, 2003).

What's a Teacher to Do?

It's been several decades since Vygotsky introduced his idea of the zone of proximal development. Like classics in literature, this idea has staying power because it speaks to a truth that we've all experienced. Having said that, it's hard to implement on a daily basis, especially when working with groups of learners. Remember that most of the early work done on zone of proximal development and instructional scaffolds was done with individual students, not small or large groups of them. Wood and Wood (1996) even note that Vygotsky's definition leaves us with the arduous task of figuring out "the nature of the guidance and the collaboration that promotes development" (p. 5).

Thankfully, a number of researchers have identified components of instructional scaffolds that have helped teachers put Vygotsky's theory into operation. For example, Ragoff (1990) validated the findings from Wood and colleagues (1976), noting that with scaffolds, "adults support children's learning by structuring the task's difficulty level, jointly participating in problem solving, focusing the learner's attention to the task and motivating the learner" (cited in Rodgers, 2004/05, p. 504). In doing so, the adult implements a number of instructional contingencies, varying the type and amount of support to ensure that the student is successful.

Maloch (2002) found that teacher scaffolds included "direct and indirect explanations, modeling, highlighting of strategies and reconstructive caps" (p. 108). Like those before her, Maloch found that varying support provided the teacher with information about new learning and needed intervention. The Maloch study also suggests a new type of scaffold, "reconstructive caps," in which the adult highlights the success of the student with the goal of encouraging the student to engage in that behavior or skill again. These reconstructive caps are one more scaffold that adults can use to facilitate student understanding.

Rodgers (2004/05) also extends our understanding of instructional scaffolds with her study of student-teacher interactions. In addition to the teacher moves we have already noted, Rodgers's data suggest that teachers should provide students with opportunities to make errors. As Elbers (1996) notes, errors are important in the learning process because they provide "occasions for various suggestions, demonstrations, or explanations" (p. 284). Provoking or noticing these errors provides the teacher with an opportunity to prompt, cue, or explain and model. In doing so, the students and teacher pay joint attention to the task and work together to reach an understanding. We've called this "productive failure" (Fisher & Frey, 2010) because these errors guide the type of instruction the student needs. Rodgers (2004/05) also notes that these errors must be balanced, because too few errors suggests that the task is too easy and scaffolds are not necessary (and thus the student is not working in the zone of proximal development), and too many errors can be "counterproductive to the learning process, because the student's engagement and contribution to the problem solving would likely diminish" (p. 526).

In addition to the recognition that errors are important, Rodgers's data suggest that support must be modulated to be effective. As we have noted, this is consistent with the "instructional contingency" recommendations made by

Wood and Wood (1996, p. 7). But Rodgers's data reflect real-time teaching, and she recognizes the difficulty in making split-second decisions about which actions to take, from modeling to demonstrating to questioning to prompting to cueing. The teachers in her study were able to make these decisions in part because they had developed a level of expertise that allowed them to recognize struggles and draw from a host of actions that they theorized would help. Perhaps even more important, as part of modulating support, Rodgers noted that the teachers had to make "decisions about what to attend to and what to ignore" (2004/05, p. 526). Again, this is a critical aspect of scaffolding student success and why it's hard to do. Parenthetically, it's also why it's hard for computers to provide expert guided instruction. It's simply very difficult to decide what to notice and then know what just-right thing to say or do to ensure that the student does cognitive work.

Guidelines for Instructional Scaffolds

Over the decades that the field has been working to clarify instructional scaffolds, a number of general guidelines have been developed. In 1983, Applebee and Langer identified five features necessary to scaffold students' understanding. As you consider each of these, notice how much they have in common with differentiated instruction and Understanding by Design (Tomlinson & McTighe, 2006):

1. **Intentionality:** The task has a clear overall purpose driving any separate activity that may contribute to the whole.
2. **Appropriateness:** Instructional tasks pose problems that can be solved with help but which students could not successfully complete on their own.
3. **Structure:** Modeling and questioning activities are structured around a model of appropriate approaches to the task and lead to a natural sequence of thought and language.
4. **Collaboration:** The teacher's response to student work recasts and expands upon the students' efforts without rejecting what they have

accomplished on their own. The teacher's primary role is collaborative rather than evaluative.

5. **Internalization:** External scaffolding for the activity is gradually withdrawn as the patterns are internalized by the students. (Applebee & Langer, 1983 as cited in Zaho & Orey, 1999, p. 6)

These five guidelines, although useful, could be a description of good teaching in general. Of course, having these guidelines in mind can help us as we plan instruction for students and pay attention to how they respond to that instruction.

In 1997, Hogan and Pressley reviewed and summarized the professional literature and identified eight essential elements of scaffolded instruction. Although the elements are not presented in any particular order, teachers can use them as general guidelines in instructional planning and implementation (Larkin, 2002):

- **Pre-engage the student and the curriculum.** The teacher considers curriculum goals and the students' needs to select appropriate tasks.
- **Establish a shared goal.** The students may become more motivated and invested in the learning process when the teacher works with each student to plan instructional goals.
- **Actively diagnose students' needs and understandings.** The teacher must be knowledgeable of content and sensitive to the students (e.g., aware of the students' background knowledge and misconceptions) to determine if they are making progress.
- **Provide tailored assistance.** This may include cueing or prompting, questioning, modeling, telling, or discussing. The teacher uses these techniques as warranted and adjusts them to meet the students' needs.
- **Maintain pursuit of the goal.** The teacher can ask questions and request clarification as well as offer praise and encouragement to help students remain focused on their goals.
- **Give feedback.** To help students learn to monitor their own progress, the teacher can summarize current progress and explicitly note behaviors that contribute to each student's success.

• **Control for frustration and risk.** The teacher can create an environment in which the students feel free to take risks with learning by encouraging them to try alternatives.

• **Assist internalization, independence, and generalization to other contexts.** This means that the teacher helps the students to be less dependent on the teacher's extrinsic signals to begin or complete a task and also provides the opportunity to practice the task in a variety of contexts.

Puntambekar and Hübscher (2005) took a different tack in their analysis of the key features of instructional scaffolds. They analyzed the key features as a theoretical construct and identified four features of scaffolds. These features shape our thinking about guided instruction, regardless of whether it is used for whole-class instruction, small-group teaching, or individualized tutoring.

1. *Intersubjectivity.* The first component necessary for instructional scaffolds to be effective involves the joint ownership of the task between the student(s) and teacher. This requires that the task be defined and redefined by the student(s) and teacher such that the student(s) begin to understand the task from the perspective of the more knowledgeable other. As Wood and colleagues (1976) noted, this involves "making it worthwhile for the learner to risk the next step" (p. 98).

2. *Ongoing diagnosis.* As we have noted throughout this book, the teacher must be continually aware of what the learner understands and still needs to learn. This requires a deep understanding of the task at hand, including the subtasks required for mastery, and a keen level of knowledge about the individual learner. As Wood and colleagues noted (1976),

> The effective tutor must have at least two theoretical models to which he must attend. One is a theory of the task or problem and how it may be completed. The other is a theory of performance characteristics of the tutee. Without both of these, he can neither generate feedback nor devise situations in which his feedback will be more appropriate for this tutee, in this task at this point in task mastering. The actual pattern of effective instruction, then, will be both task and tutee dependent, the

requirements of the tutorial being generated by the interaction of the tutor's two theories. (p. 97)

3. *Dialogic and interactive.* A third feature of learning scaffolds relates to the conversation that the student(s) and teacher have as part of the learning situation. This is not a time for a monologue, but rather a dialogue in which the teacher monitors student understanding and progress. It requires a fairly sophisticated feedback system in which the teacher is regularly checking for understanding and collecting assessment information.

4. *Fading.* The final theoretical feature requires that the teacher fade the support provided to the learner(s). In Vygotskian terms, this occurs when the learner has reached *internalization.* Vygotsky (1978) hypothesized that cognition first occurs between people (interpsychological) before moving to intrapsychological (within one's own self). Without fading, this process of internalization cannot happen; students become "prompt-dependent," not independent. In educational terminology, we think of this as reaching automaticity (LaBerge & Samuels, 1974), which we have already discussed in terms of freeing working memory to focus on understanding.

Again, we find these guidelines helpful in planning good instruction, but they're still fairly general. Here's another general idea worth remembering: the intent of the scaffold, or guided instruction, is to create situations that build students' knowledge so that they can apply, evaluate, and create—those elusive critical thinking skills first described by Benjamin Bloom in 1956 and updated by Anderson and Krathwohl in 2001 to reflect the kinds of learning we think about today (see Figure 1.1).

Taking Action with Scaffolds

Although scaffolds can result in higher levels of student achievement, providing them is a very demanding form of instruction (Pressley, Hogan, Wharton-McDonald, Mistretta, & Ettenberger, 1996). Lipscomb, Swanson, and West (2004) identify a number of specific challenges that must be addressed if

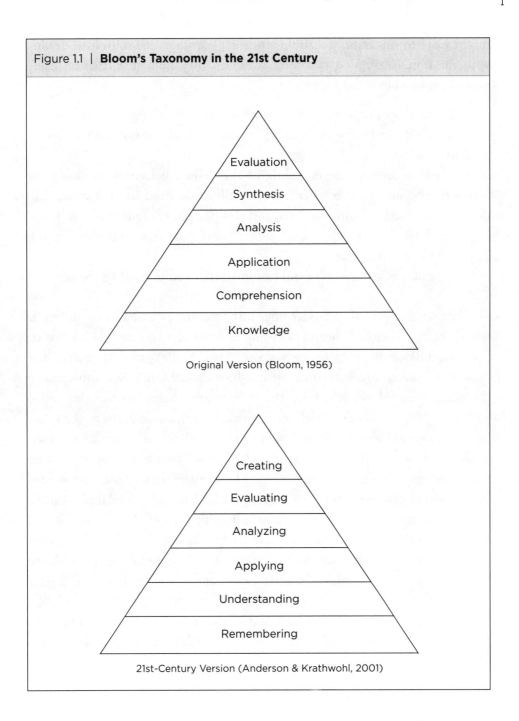

Figure 1.1 | **Bloom's Taxonomy in the 21st Century**

Original Version (Bloom, 1956)

21st-Century Version (Anderson & Krathwohl, 2001)

teachers are to successfully scaffold students' learning. In addition to dealing with the time-consuming nature of scaffolds, they note that teachers using them have to address the following:

- Potential for misjudging the zone of proximal development, because success hinges on identifying the area that is just beyond but not too far beyond students' abilities
- Need for appropriate modeling of the desired behaviors, strategies, or activities, because if the teacher has not fully considered the individual student's needs, predilections, interests, and abilities, the scaffolds will not help
- Need to give up control as fading occurs, because scaffolds are not intended to be permanent
- Lack of specific examples and tips in teacher's editions of textbooks

These challenges can be overcome. Just listen in as Ms. Conroy interacts with her class. They have been examining cell structure, starting with building background knowledge from the website "How Stuff Works" (http://science.howstuffworks.com/cellular-microscopic-biology/cell.htm). She shows them the video about blood cells from the website and shares her thinking aloud with them. As part of her modeling, she makes connections between the information about red blood cells and the plant and animal cells they have already studied. She also asks herself questions and records these questions for later investigation. Following her modeling, Ms. Conroy uses whole-class guided instruction to determine students' level of understanding and readiness for the lab. She starts by asking them to draw a bacterial cell of their choice and to label the internal structures accordingly. They take out their dry-erase boards and get to work. Bradley chooses to draw the *E. coli* bacterium and has labeled the cell membrane, cytoplasm, flagella, DNA, and mitochondria. Noticing his error (bacteria do not have mitochondria), Ms. Conroy reviews the work of a few other students to see if they have added structures that do not belong. Like several other students, Chelsea has incorrectly included Golgi bodies in her *Streptococcus pneumoniae* cell.

Ms. Conroy interrupts the class to say, "Remember, these are bacteria. They're more basic than human cells. Check your work." Several students look at their dry-erase boards and remove incorrect structures. Bradley does not, so Ms. Conroy says to him, "Think about each structure you've labeled and if it is appropriate for a bacterial cell." Bradley doesn't change anything on his board, so Ms. Conroy says, "I know that *E. coli*, as a bacteria, has a membrane. That's a common feature, as cells need a structure to contain their contents. And cells carry DNA. Well done. Ah, yes, and you have the flagella, a telltale sign of bacteria. Not all bacteria have them, but they're pretty common. What about the other structures you've labeled?"

At this point, Bradley recognizes his error and erases *mitochondria*. While doing so, he says to Ms. Conroy, "You never just tell us the answer; you make us think for ourselves." And there it is—the interaction that changed Bradley's understanding of cellular structure. Of course, it won't always happen this fast. But when we're careful and we pay attention to students and their developing understanding, saying or doing the just-right thing will ensure that *they* do the cognitive work, not the teacher. After all, we've completed our K–12 schooling; it's time for our students to do so.

The remainder of this book focuses on specific tools that you can use to guide students to greater levels of understanding. Taken together, these teacher moves, from questioning to checking for understanding to prompting, cueing, explaining, and modeling, provide a structure to realize the vision Vygotsky had for education in which students *become themselves* through their interactions with members of the learning community.

2

Questioning to Check for Understanding

Most of us were introduced to the concept of open-ended and closed questions when we were in teacher preparation programs. We were taught that an open-ended question was likely to draw out a longer response than a closed one. By turning a closed question that can be answered with a specific piece of information ("What answer did you get for number 5?") to an open-ended one that allows for more than one response ("How did you get the answer for number 5?"), we can provoke more insightful commentary from students. But open-ended and closed questions describe student response formats. Although these are important considerations for bolstering engagement, they don't fully address the teacher's purpose for asking either question in the first place.

Checking for understanding is foundational to guided instruction, as the student's response provides the teacher with a decision-making point: do I need to further scaffold this learner's understanding? In the next chapters we'll explore how and when to scaffold, but for now let's stay on this point. At various places throughout a lesson, we need to check for understanding so we can plan for future instruction. These periodic checks allow us to determine the following:

- What the learner knows
- What the learner doesn't know
- The extent to which a learner is linking background knowledge with newer concepts
- Whether there are fundamental misconceptions that are getting in the way of understanding

A core assumption is that the things a learner says and does make perfect sense *to the learner,* based on what she knows and doesn't know at that moment in time. This is a big assumption, because as teachers we tend to be more comfortable with assessing the rightness or wrongness of an answer, as opposed to its source. Quite frankly, it's easier to simply evaluate whether the student was able to play a game Doug calls "Guess What's in the Teacher's Brain." Embracing an assumption of partial understanding is more difficult, especially because it demands rapid analysis, formulation of a hypothesis, and then creation of a plan for instructional response. In guided instruction, these decisions must occur in seconds in order to provide a prompt or cue.

In his book *Blink,* Malcolm Gladwell (2005) devotes a chapter to the concept of "thin slicing," the ability "to find patterns in situations and behavior on very narrow slices of experience" (p. 23). He notes that many professions have unique terms for this—in basketball it is called "court sense," and in the military it is referred to as *coup d'oeil* ("power of the glance"). In teaching, it's called instructional decision making. In many ways, this is the art and science of teaching in that it combines the knowledge that comes from closely observed learning events with the technical tools and research that we use daily in our classrooms. One without the other is not enough.

Much of the information that we gather during guided instruction comes in the form of questioning. It is important to note that the mere existence of a question mark doesn't automatically indicate that the teacher is checking for understanding. As we will describe in more detail throughout this book, it's the intent that matters. A cue or a prompt can be delivered in the form of a question, but it's still a cue or a prompt. However, when checking for understanding, we are posing a question for the purpose of figuring out what students know and don't know. Without the intent to analyze, hypothesize, and respond, the power of the question is unrealized.

Intention in Checking for Understanding

A variety of means are available for checking for understanding, including analysis of student products in written work, spoken language, projects, performances, and assessments (Fisher & Frey, 2007). In guided instruction, questioning is the predominant tool for determining what students know. It is important to recognize that what is done with the question is essential. Consider this exchange:

Teacher: What is a nocturnal animal?

Student: An animal that stays awake at night.

Teacher: Good. What is a diurnal animal?

We would argue that the teacher is quizzing, not questioning. In this case, the teacher is running through a list of technical vocabulary (*nocturnal, diurnal*) to determine how closely the student's answer matches the book definition. Contrast the preceding exchange with this scenario:

Teacher: What is a nocturnal animal?

Student: An animal that stays awake at night.

Teacher: Tell me more about that. Does a nocturnal animal have special characteristics?

Student: Well, it doesn't sleep a lot.

And so a misconception reveals itself. This student is making a completely reasonable answer, *based on what he knows and doesn't know at this time*, and incorrectly assumes that nocturnal animals are sleep-deprived. The teacher didn't teach this, but the student believes it nonetheless. It is the follow-up probe that makes the difference. The teacher's intent in using a question is to uncover, not test. And here's where the teacher uses his thin-slicing abilities to make his next instructional decision. He could say the following:

Teacher: I'm thinking of those pictures we saw of the great horned owl and the slow loris in the daytime and at night. Does your answer still work? [a prompt to activate background knowledge]

Alternatively, the teacher might say this:

Teacher: Let's take a look on page 35 and reread the second paragraph. Does the author agree or disagree with you? [a cue to shift the learner's attention to a source of information]

In both cases, the teacher considered what the student knew and did not know and followed up with a prompt or a cue to scaffold the student's understanding. The ability to do this is not innate—we do not believe that some people are "born" teachers. But too often we don't recognize where the learner might get stuck. There's even a name for this phenomenon. It's called the "expert blind spot," and it describes the inability of inexperienced educators to understand the stance of novice learners (their students) in learning a new concept (Nathan & Petrosino, 2003). In particular, experts tend to overestimate the relative ease of a task. That's actually good news for all of us involved in education, because we can turn that expertise into scaffolds for students. The ability to check for understanding, hypothesize, and then follow with a cue or a prompt can be learned through a combination of experience and purposeful attention.

Purposeful Attention to Misconceptions in Guided Instruction

Research on the expert blind spot contains advice on how to move beyond it, and it is no surprise that the advice rests on drawing purposeful attention to the misconception. When teachers are made aware of this phenomenon, and this is further coupled with developmental and pedagogical knowledge, the blind spot grows smaller (Kelley & Jacoby, 1996). This finding is consistent with what is known about the effect of misconceptions on the learning of children and adolescents. When the teacher anticipates the misconception and draws purposeful attention to it, accurate learning can occur (Bereiter & Scardamalia, 1992). Much of this process happens through guided instruction.

Misconceptions have been documented in all content areas but are especially dominant in mathematics and science. For example, many elementary students do not see the relationship between the source of light and the color of an object. Therefore, they do not understand that the appearance of a blue sky is due to the way the light is scattered through the process of dispersion. The underlying misconception is that white light is just one color—white—rather than consisting of a range of colors that travel at different frequencies. This misconception is usually addressed through labs involving glass prisms and rainbows, so that students can witness how the colors of white light can be refracted into the spectrum. Third grade teacher Ms. Wainwright had led her students through several such experiments, but she also knew that this misconception tends to persist. During guided instruction with her students, she had the following conversation. Notice how she uses questions to probe for a misconception:

Ms. Wainwright: We've been studying about light in science. Let's start by talking about what you know so far. I'll write it down on the chart. Rebekah, can you begin? Tell me one thing you know about light.

Rebekah: We learned that the light we see outside comes from the sun.

Ms. Wainwright [writing]: That's a great start. Tell me more about the sun. How would you describe it to someone?

Rebekah: Well, it's big and yellow, and it's in the sky.

Ms. Wainwright: That's an interesting description. Let's take that apart. You said it's yellow. How do you know that?

Rebekah: I can look up and I see it. You can't look at it for long 'cause it'll hurt your eyes.

Ms. Wainwright: Are there other ways you know the sun is yellow?

Rebekah: When you draw a sun you always make it yellow.

Ms. Wainwright: What if an astronaut were drawing a picture of the sun when she was in space? Would she draw it yellow?

Rebekah: Yep, 'cause that's what it looks like.

Ms. Wainwright: So even in space the sun is yellow?

Rebekah: Yep, yellow.

This short exchange unearthed exactly what Ms. Wainwright had anticipated—despite some good instruction, Rebekah persisted in believing that the sun itself was yellow, as opposed to understanding that it appears to be yellow due to the refraction of white light by Earth's atmosphere. Based on Rebekah's responses, as well as similar conversations with other learners, the teacher knew that she would need to do more direct instruction to dispel this misconception. Her next lesson would consist of photographs of the sun taken from Earth and from space, direct explanation about the misconception, and another lab designed to challenge students' reasoning by asking them to investigate why clouds appear to be white, not yellow. "I have to keep asking questions to check for their understanding," Ms. Wainwright later said, "but I'm not looking for them to regurgitate the information. When I ask questions that require them to explain and justify, I find out where their scientific knowledge ends and naïve understandings take over."

What Do You Do with Their Answers?

As Ms. Wainwright demonstrated, asking questions to check for understanding should do more than merely sort right answers from wrong ones. As a matter of intent, questions posed to check on student understanding should *feed forward* to modify future instruction (Fisher & Frey, 2009b). This is part of a multipronged approach to formative assessment that includes feeding up and feeding back. *Feeding up* occurs at the onset, with clearly established purposes for learning, including content and language objectives. These purposes are specific to the individual lesson and are not restatements of the standards, which are much broader and usually require multiple experiences. For instance, a content purpose in an 8th grade social studies lesson is to identify examples of religious and class discrimination against Irish workers in the first half of the 19th century, and a language purpose is to use three examples of evidence of such discrimination in a written summary.

The second component of a formative assessment system, *feedback*, is more familiar and consists of responses to student work. Many times feedback is written, but it can also be achieved verbally. It is important to recognize that the quality of the response affects what a student is able to do next. The ubiquitous "*awk*" scrawled in red pen in the margin of an essay doesn't provide construc-tive feedback for a student writer and instead merely critiques the sentence or idea construction as "awkward." Decidedly unhelpful comments like this end up in the trash can, leaving students frustrated with how to proceed and teachers bewildered by their students' unwillingness to make another attempt. Instead, a host of studies on the nature and effectiveness of feedback suggest that it should be—

• Descriptive, rather than evaluative
• Focused on the task, rather than the student
• Improvement-oriented, rather than achievement-oriented (Hattie & Timperley, 2007)

The third element of a formative assessment system is *feeding forward*. Much of what the teacher does through guided instruction is intended to feed forward to modify future instruction. Some of this feeding forward must occur during subsequent lessons, as when Ms. Wainwright made plans for a new lesson on light based on tightly held misconceptions that persisted. In other cases, feeding forward happens more rapidly, as when the teacher directed his student's attention back to a passage in the book about nocturnal animals. In this last example, the questioning led to the use of a cue. Based on the stu-dent's response, he was provided with a cue that shifted his attention to an information source. If the student is then able to construct a correct response, the teacher can move on. If the child still does not realize that many nocturnal animals have unique characteristics such as large eyes that enable them to see in the dark, then the teacher reclaims cognitive control by offering further direct explanation and modeling (see Chapter 5).

Figure 2.1 illustrates a decision-making flowchart for making instructional decisions based on student responses. Questions within guided instruction are a springboard for further questions, prompts, and cues. When these scaffolds are insufficient, it signals to the teacher that further modeling is needed before the learning progression can continue. We recognize that real discussions are far more complex than the illustration suggests, and we are not suggesting that

Figure 2.1 | **Instructional Decision-Making Tree**

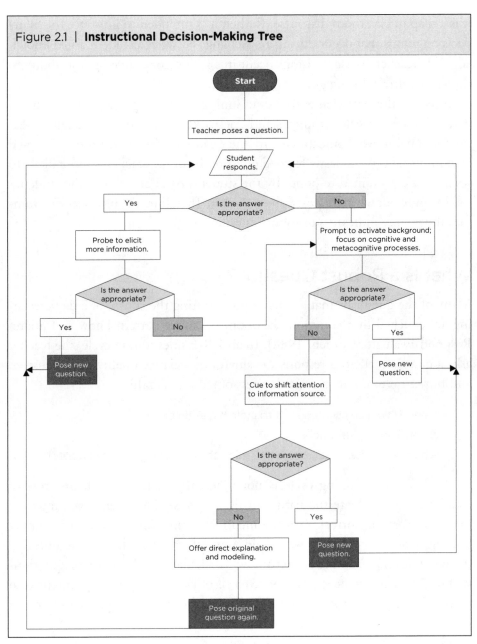

Source: Frey, N., & Fisher, D. (2010). Identifying instructional moves during guided learning. *The Reading Teacher*, 64(2). © 2010 by the International Reading Association. Used with permission.

it is a map of classroom discourse. Rather, it is intended to illustrate the many decision points that occur during an exchange between a student and a knowledgeable teacher. These decisions occur in a split second, making the ability to thin-slice critical during guided instruction.

Intent is the first element of questioning, and the purpose should be to determine what a student knows and doesn't know in order to make the next instructional move. You can see why the quality of the question that is posed is so important. A carelessly formed question from the teacher is more likely to result in a constrained response by the student. After all, it's not the student's job to figure out why you posed the question. Therefore, the next section examines the quality indicators of robust questions.

What Is a Robust Question?

Many of the questions that a teacher poses during the course of a day's teaching are couched in a common classroom discourse pattern know as Initiate-Respond-Evaluate (Cazden, 1988). In an I-R-E questioning cycle, the teacher asks a question, elicits a response, evaluates the relative quality of the answer, and moves on to the next cycle. It goes something like this:

> **Teacher:** How many sides does a triangle have? (Initiate)
> **Student:** Three. (Respond)
> **Teacher:** Good. (Evaluate) How many sides does a rectangle have? (Initiate)

An I-R-E questioning cycle is not inherently bad. After all, one role of a teacher is to evaluate the nature of the response. However, if the intent is merely to sort the correct from the incorrect, evaluation is reduced to simply keeping score. In addition, we would argue that the quality of the question in the preceding example is pretty low, particularly if the types of questions within the exchange never rise above recall of facts. Further, if the intent is to control rather than probe, this questioning technique is not going to result in much benefit for either the teacher or the student.

On the other hand, a robust question is one that is crafted to find out more about what students know, how they use information, and where any confusion may lie. A robust question sets up subsequent instruction because it provides the information you need to further prompt, cue, or explain and model. In particular, you want to determine the extent to which students are beginning to use the knowledge they are learning. In keeping with a Gradual Release of Responsibility model, the expectation is that students are still at an early stage and are not yet at the level of mastery. If students are able to answer robust questions thoroughly, then that is an indication that they are ready to further refine their understanding in the company of peers, especially through productive group work (Frey et al., 2009). We have grouped the major types of questions used in guided instruction into categories. Some questions elicit information, some invite students to link previous knowledge to new information, and some encourage further elaboration or clarification. In addition, robust questioning requires students to problem solve and to speculate.

Elicitation Questions

These form the backbone of questioning for guided instruction because they draw on skills and concepts that have been previously taught. These foundational questions provide the teacher with a baseline from which to work. A student who is unable to respond to an elicitation question is likely to need more direct explanation and modeling. Elicitation questions can focus on finite knowledge ("What is the name of the protective case a caterpillar makes as it becomes a butterfly?"). Conversely, an elicitation question might require application-level knowledge ("Why does the chrysalis need to be hard?"). The variable here is what has been initially taught during a focus lesson. That lesson may have been composed of what Bloom (1956) describes as knowledge- and comprehension-level understandings, or perhaps it consisted of application- or synthesis-level knowledge. When asking an elicitation question, the teacher's purpose is to gauge what the student has retained through instruction to this point.

For example, after 9th grade English teacher Kelly Johnson introduced her students to persuasive techniques using direct explanation and modeling, she asked them a series of elicitation questions. As she displayed print advertisements on the screen, she instructed her students to identify the techniques used. She showed them a popular ad from the Marines that read, "The few. The proud. The Marines." Her students correctly identified this as including a "glittering generality." Because she had modeled providing the rationale, she asked them to justify their answer. Olivia said, "It's got really powerful emotional words in it, like *proud*."

Elicitation questions can also be posed to unearth misconceptions. When 5th grade teacher Zach Eloy asks a small group of his mathematics students to estimate their answers before calculating the equation $3/8 \times 1/2 = $ _____, he is listening for whether they anticipate that the answer will be larger or smaller than the numbers they began with. Although he has introduced this concept using a think-aloud process so his students could witness how he uses his mathematical reasoning, he is not sure whether this group has yet reached this understanding. His purpose for posing this elicitation question is to see if these learners still cling to the misconception that multiplication always results in a larger number.

Divergent Questions

These questions require students to couple previously taught information with new knowledge. There's a ladder effect going on here. Much like a person using a lower step to hoist himself onto a higher one, some types of knowledge are built in a similar fashion. The Reading Recovery program refers to this as using knowledge "on the run"—that is, applying previously learned information to figure out something new (Clay, 2001). When kindergarten teacher Ming Li asks her students to transform the word *goose* to *loose* using the magnetic letters she has arranged on the whiteboard, she is asking them a divergent question, and she is observing how they are using what they know about the letter-sound relationships and the way words work to construct a new word.

Elaboration Questions

Some robust questions come as a follow-up probe to an initial question. An elaboration question is used to find out more about a student's reasoning. In particular, these questions invite students to extend their response by adding ideas. For example, 11th grade chemistry teacher Al Montoya pauses at the desk of Edress and reads the student's lab sheet over his shoulder. Mr. Montoya points to the third question, which asks Edress to make a prediction about what will occur when a piece of zinc metal is added to a salt solution and an acidic one. Noting that Edress has written, "I don't think anything will happen to the metal," Mr. Montoya says, "Tell me more about this prediction. Why do you think nothing will happen to the zinc?" By asking Edress to elaborate on his response, Mr. Montoya is probing the reasoning his student is using to support this prediction.

Clarification Questions

As with elaboration questions, which often come after an initial response, clarification questions invite students to extend their thinking by requiring them to provide a clear explanation. A clarification may be genuine, as when the teacher truly doesn't understand a student's response. In other cases, the clarification question is used to further expose student understanding about a concept. In her 7th grade social studies classroom, Cindy Seymour routinely asks clarification questions during guided instruction. "I always remind [students] that they need to 'think like a historian,' so they have to provide evidence. 'Because' is a big word around here." During guided instruction on the narratives of formerly enslaved people in their Southern state, Ms. Seymour asks her students to draw a powerful image of the passage their collaborative learning group read and discussed. When Brandi displays her group's drawing of a whip, Ms. Seymour poses a clarification question, asking them to provide a direct quote from the reading.

Heuristic Questions

The term *heuristic* may be unfamiliar, but what it represents is not. A heuristic is an informal problem-solving technique, sometimes described as a rule of thumb. Our guess is that you have developed heuristics for where to park your car at the mall, choosing a checkout line at the grocery store, and hosting a large family gathering. It's likely that you did not learn these techniques formally, but instead developed them over the years through experience and conversation with others. In classrooms, heuristics refer to the academic problem-solving techniques students use to arrive at a solution. For example, a commonly taught heuristic in mathematics is to draw a visual representation of a word problem to visualize the operation. When 1st grade teacher Marilen Cervantes asks her mathematics students how they keep track of objects they are counting, she is posing a heuristic question. When 10th grade world history teacher George Boyle asks a student to use a graphic organizer of her choice to show the political alliances during the imprisonment of Mary, Queen of Scots, by Elizabeth I, he is posing a heuristic question.

Inventive Questions

An inventive question requires students to use their knowledge to speculate or create. Again, the emphasis is on using information that students have been recently taught in order to create something new. Fourth grade teacher Beth Kowalski asks Ronaldo, who has just finished the latest installment of the *Time Warp Trio* series by Jon Scieszka and Lane Smith, to make a recommendation about who might like the book. This inventive question requires Ronaldo to consider what he knows about the series and to combine that with newer knowledge on developing book recommendations. Twelfth grade English teacher John Goodwin asks Shaudi to tell him how Ayn Rand's *Anthem* (2009) helps her to answer the school's essential question, "Can money buy happiness?" Like Ronaldo, Shaudi has to integrate what she knows about different topics and situations to answer the question.

Figure 2.2 presents a summary of the various types of questions. In addition to these, there are specific types of questions that relate to texts that students are reading. We'll explore these four types of questions next, then turn our attention to creating a system for using questions.

Question-Answer Relationships

Question-Answer Relationships (QAR) is a system designed to teach students how to locate and formulate answers based on specific types of questions often asked about a piece of text (Raphael, 1982, 1984). This system, which has been

Figure 2.2	**Types of Questions to Determine Student Knowledge**	
Type of Question	**Purpose**	**Examples**
Elicitation	To unearth misconceptions and check for factual knowledge	• Who...? • What...? • When...? • Where...? • Why...? • How...?
Divergent	To discover how the student uses existing knowledge to formulate new understandings	• Why does water look blue in a lake, but clear in a glass? • Do good governments and bad governments have anything in common?
Elaboration	To extend the length and complexity of the response	• Can you tell me more about that?
Clarification	To gain further details	• Can you show me where you found that information? • Why did you choose that answer?
Heuristic	To determine the learner's ability to problem solve	• How would you set up this word problem? • If I were looking for information about spring in this book, where could I look? • How do you know when you have run out of ways to answer this question?
Inventive	To stimulate imaginative thought	• If you could, what advice would you give to Napoleon at the Battle of Waterloo? • Who would you recommend this book to?

Frey, N., & Fisher, D. (2010). Identifying instructional moves during guided learning. *The Reading Teacher*, 64(2). © 2010 by the International Reading Association. Adapted with permission.

shown to positively affect student test scores (Raphael & Au, 2005), consists of four types of questions.

The first two types are both explicit questions, meaning that the answer can be found in the text. *Right There* questions contain wording that comes directly from the text, with an answer often found in a single sentence. *Think and Search* questions are also derived directly from the text, but the answer must be formulated across more than one sentence.

The other two types of questions are both implicit, meaning that the answer cannot be located directly in the text and must be formulated by connecting what the reader knows with the text. *Author and You* is an implicit question that requires readers to use both information learned in the text and their own background knowledge to answer. The final type of implicit question is *On Your Own*, which requires readers to use prior knowledge to answer. In this final case, the text may or may not be needed (Raphael, 1986). It is helpful to think of these as "book" and "brain" questions. *Right There* and *Think and Search* are book questions, because the answers can be found directly in the text. On the other hand, *Author and You* and *On Your Own* questions are brain questions, in that readers must consider what they know as well as what they have learned from the reading.

Struggling readers often have difficulty in making decisions about how to answer questions. We've all seen a student futilely searching a text passage for an answer that simply is not there. These same students will often choose a direct quote from the passage even when it is not the correct answer. The QAR approach "clarifies how students can approach the task of reading texts and answering questions" (Raphael, 1986, p. 517). QAR teaches students to locate and justify answers by showing them how to identify four types of questions. Learning to identify a question type and its relationship to the text helps students build comprehension by monitoring and clarifying their reading.

Of course, students need instructional scaffolds if they are to use QAR effectively. This scaffolding should start with teachers introducing the question types, if students don't already know them or haven't used them in a while. Figure 2.3 shows a chart that can be used to introduce students to the definitions of each question type. Remember, these scaffolds must be faded so that students get practice with using the tools effectively and independently.

Figure 2.3	**Question-Answer Relationships**		
Question Type	**Description**	**Question Stems**
In the Text (Book Questions)		
Right There	Words in the question and answer are directly stated in the text. The question is explicit, and the words or phrases can be found within one sentence.	• How many...? • Who is...? • Where is...? • What is...?
Think and Search	Information is in the text, but readers must think and make connections between passages in the text.	• The main idea is...? • What caused...? • What happened when...?
In My Head (Brain Questions)		
Author and You	Readers need to think about what they already know, what the author tells them in the text, and how these fit together.	• The author implies...? • The passage suggests...? • The author's attitude...?
On Your Own	Requires the reader to use prior knowledge to answer. The text may or may not be needed.	• In your own opinion...? • Based on your experience...? • What would you do if...?

Source: From *After School Content Literacy Project for California* (p. 186), by D. Fisher, N. Frey, and L. Young, 2007, Sacramento: California Department of Education. Reprinted with permission.

Once students have been introduced to the question types and have had modeling and practice with them, the questions are useful in checking for understanding. For example, while reading the social studies text, the members of Justin's group created questions that would guide their conversation about the text following the reading. Justin turned the headings into questions, while other members of his group used various other question-generating techniques. During their discussion, the students agreed on the question type and used that information to formulate their responses. Consider the following student-generated questions from their reading about ancient civilizations:

- Why are the early humans important for us to know about? [Think and Search]
- Who were the early humans? [Right There]
- How were the early humans discovered? [Think and Search]
- How would we adapt to their life? [Author and You]
- What were the Ice Ages? [Right There]
- What do people today need to survive? [On Your Own]

Although reading and discussing the text is important, the questions students generate allow the teacher to check for their understanding of both the content of what they read as well as their ability to find answers to questions.

In addition, teachers can use QAR to check for understanding of groups of students. When they do not respond appropriately, QAR has a built-in system for providing prompts. Mr. Bradshaw was reading aloud from a biography, *The Man Who Ran Faster Than Everyone: The Story of Tom Longboat* (Batten, 2002). Pausing, he asked the class to talk with a partner about what they knew about the Olympics. After two minutes, he interrupted their discussion and began reading:

> The ancient story goes that when the Persians invaded Greece in 490 B.C., landing near the coastal village of Marathon, they outnumbered the Greeks six to one and seemed certain to win the battle. But the ferocious defenders slaughtered 6,400 of the Persian enemy and sent the rest fleeing in their ships. A Greek messenger named Pheidippides, so the story continues, was dispatched to Athens to deliver the glad news of the unexpected victory. Pheidippides raced the 24 miles from Marathon to

Athens, pausing for nothing—not for rest nor water nor a change of sandals. He rushed to the ruling chamber in Athens, looked into the worried faces of the elders, and summoned the breath to shout: "Rejoice! We conquer!" His duty done, Pheidippides dropped dead. (p. 23)

After the teacher completed the section, he asked the class a few questions. Consider the conversation the class had as Mr. Bradshaw used questions to check for understanding and plan his guided instruction:

Mr. Bradshaw: Angelica, what does the author mean by "defenders"?

Angelica: People who protected things, like their land and stuff.

Mr. Bradshaw: Class, do you agree? Thumbs up or down. [All the students have thumbs up.] Trevor, who won the war?

Trevor: It says right in the text that the Greeks did, but I also know that from history.

Mr. Bradshaw: Right on. Class? [All the students have thumbs up.] Andrew, describe the journey of the messenger.

Andrew: He died.

Mr. Bradshaw: Sad, but true. And along the way? Devon, tell us more.

Devon: He ran 24 miles, from Marathon to Athens. He didn't stop for nothing. He just ran.

Mr. Bradshaw: Class? [About three-fourths of the students have their thumbs up.] Oh, some disagreement. Tara, care to add?

Tara: He did all that, but it was to get the message through. He didn't have no cell phone or anything, but he had to get that message to the people in Athens.

Mr. Bradshaw: Yes, that's true. The message to the elders was an important one, and, given the times, there wasn't really another way. But why does the author say "the story continues"? Why that language, Caroline?

Caroline: That's what authors do. They continue the story.

Mr. Bradshaw: Class? [Nearly all of the students have their thumbs up, indicating they agree with the Caroline's statement.] Ah, I see that we'll need to focus a bit more on author's craft and author's intent. Remember, every word matters. There has to be a reason why the author says this. Let's read on and see what we can find out.

Quality Questioning

We've discussed a number of question types and two different systems for generating questions. Now, let's focus on the questioning process. Implementing such a process provides clues for you to use to guide the learner through prompts, cues, and explanations and modeling. Without a process, questioning can become random and will not result in learning. Without a process, teachers create questions on the spot, and these questions are often lower-level recall questions that do not provide opportunities to clarify and extend students' understanding. This is a problem because we know that students attend to information based on how they are asked about that information. In other words, if they're asked lots of recall questions, they learn to read for that type of information. For example, Reynolds and Anderson (1982) showed that text information relevant to questions was learned better than text information irrelevant to the type of questions being asked. Yes, the type of questions asked does matter.

We are also reminded of Durkin's (1978–79) findings that teachers rely primarily on questioning to *teach* comprehension. Questions don't teach understanding; teachers do. The responses to questions we ask should guide our interactions with students and help us determine how to respond, either with prompts, cues, explanations, or modeling. Remember, we have to do something with the responses we get to the great questions we ask; it's not enough to simply ask students questions.

We are particularly fond of the five-step questioning process that Walsh and Sattes (2005) describe as Questioning and Understanding to Improve Learning and Thinking, or QUILT:

> **Stage 1: Prepare the Question**
> * Identify instructional purpose
> * Determine content focus
> * Select cognitive level
> * Consider wording and syntax

Stage 2: Present the Question
- Indicate response format
- Ask the question
- Select respondent

Stage 3: Prompt Student Responses
- Pause after asking question
- Assist nonrespondents
- Pause following student response

Stage 4: Process Student Responses
- Provide appropriate feedback
- Expand and use correct responses
- Elicit student reactions and questions

Stage 5: Reflect on Questioning Practice
- Analyze questions
- Map respondent selection
- Evaluate student response patterns
- Examine teacher and student reactions (p. vi)

Notice how the questions should be prepared in advance. That's not to say that a perfect question won't arise from an interaction between the teacher and the student, but having questions ready ensures that the teacher is prepared. It also ensures that we know why we're asking a specific question and how we expect learners to respond. Further, as noted in Stage 1, the questions should reflect the instructional purpose and content focus of the lesson. This helps us keep on track and prevents us from taking interesting excursions, or tangents, that do not relate to the topic at hand.

As noted in Stage 2, when the question is presented, learners need to be given a response system. Do they talk with a partner? Or do they write or raise their hands? In addition, Stage 2 serves as a reminder to notify the students who will be expected to respond. As we have learned from the research on Teacher Expectations and Student Achievement (Los Angeles County Office of

Education, 2009), students need equal response opportunities if they are going to be accountable for the information and receive attention from the teacher. There are a number of ways to ensure that students experience an equal opportunity to respond, ranging from randomly calling on students using Popsicle sticks or the attendance roster to inclusive response opportunities such as dry-erase boards and audience-response systems (also known as clickers, with each student using a device to answer the question).

Prompting is also an important part of a questioning system. As noted in Stage 3, the teacher has to pause for the student to answer. TESA, in the category of latency, suggests that the teacher wait at least five seconds after asking a question to see if the student will respond before prompting or moving to another student. The TESA research also suggests that the teacher should wait two to three additional seconds after the student has finished speaking to provide an opportunity for the student to elaborate on the response. In addition, as part of Stage 3, the teacher assists nonrespondents, a skill that is covered in the following chapters.

In Stage 4, the teacher processes the student response. This stage involves feedback, prompting, and cueing. Again, the following chapters include guidance for exactly this aspect of the questioning system: what to do when students respond, whether or not the response is correct or appropriate.

Finally, in Stage 5, the teacher reflects on questioning practices. This stage includes analyzing the questions to determine if they were effective in checking for understanding and guiding instruction. It also involves an analysis of student response patterns and reactions.

Taken together, this system of questioning provides the teacher with an approach to checking for understanding with the goal of addressing student needs through guided instruction. When we're at our best, we guide students by saying and doing the just-right thing to get students to engage in cognitive work. This guidance requires that we link instruction with student responses to the questions we ask.

Summing Up

The core assumption in guided instruction is that student responses provide the teacher with insight into what the learner knows and does not know at that moment in time. A knowledgeable teacher—one who possesses both content knowledge and a deep understanding of how a novice learner approaches a new concept—rapidly hypothesizes the learner's current state and responds with prompts, cues, or direct explanation and modeling when needed. The ability to expose student understanding or partial understanding requires anticipating misconceptions and posing robust questions. These robust questions are purposeful and are designed to elicit information about previously taught concepts and to encourage linking previous knowledge to new. In some cases, further elaboration or clarification questions are needed to unearth student knowledge. Robust questions can also be used to give the teacher insight as to how a student solves an academic problem, and inventive questions invite students to speculate.

It is useful for students to learn about questions in order to locate information in their heads and in their materials. The Question-Answer Relationship instructional routine is especially relevant for showing students how they know the things they know. *Right There* and *Think and Search* questions are explicit, and the answers can be found within the text. On the other hand, *Author and You* and *On Your Own* questions require the learner to synthesize knowledge found both within and outside of the text. Just as these techniques can be taught to students, so can other techniques be used by teachers to improve questioning. These techniques include planning questions in advance, providing wait time, and using follow-up probes to encourage further response. Most important, student responses should be analyzed in order to plan both immediate and subsequent instruction. It is this diagnostic intent that lifts questioning from merely keeping a tally of correct and incorrect answers to more sophisticated guided instruction. Merely asking questions doesn't equal guided instruction. But when the questions are robust and purposeful, and are used to hypothesize student knowledge, the prompting and cueing that follow scaffold student learning.

3

Prompting for Cognitive and Metacognitive Processes

Not long ago, Doug was working with a high school senior named David who was struggling to complete an essay addressing the following question: "What is race, and does it matter?" David's English class had spent several weeks reading and discussing informational and fictional works related to this topic. David's English teacher had also spent lots of time talking about the construction of a formal essay, as well as how to cite works using the Modern Language Association (MLA) protocols. However, David was stymied by the size of the task and beginning to panic as the deadline loomed. Doug scheduled time in David's class to provide additional guided instruction for the student.

Doug began by asking David some questions to ascertain what he already knew about the topic and the task. He discovered that David had a clear idea about how he wanted to approach the essay question: "I want to talk about race and education. Like that slaves weren't allowed to learn to read and write, because that was dangerous." He went on to explain that he had read about historic laws that prohibited anyone from teaching literacy to an enslaved person, under threat of whipping. However, David was less sure about how to organize his ideas into a formal paper. Based on David's answers, Doug began a series of prompts intended to focus his knowledge and his ability to self-assess regarding essay writing.

He began by prompting David to list what he knew about the essay requirements. David told Doug he was supposed to use the elements of argumentation—ethos, pathos, and logos—to support the position. Doug drew a series of boxes on a sheet of lined paper and labeled them with these elements, saying, "Let's list the examples you want to discuss in your paper and put them into the category that fits best." Over the next several minutes, David provided further information about the Little Rock Nine, high school students who were harassed for enrolling in a white high school in 1957. He showed Doug a photograph of white students and parents screaming at an African American student as she entered the building. Military police flanked the girl. "That's really powerful," Doug replied. "What do you believe that's an example of? There are some categories that aren't completed yet." David looked at the list and the photograph and replied that he could use this as pathos, because of its emotional pull.

After a few more minutes of discussion, Doug prompted again. "We need to transfer these ideas to the planning sheet your teacher gave you. That will give you an idea of where the holes are in your essay." As David filled in the planning sheet and wrote his thesis statement, Doug again prompted, "Is your reader going to understand your position based on the thesis you've written? Read it again and think about it from the reader's standpoint." After rereading it, Doug and David refined the thesis statement to reflect the evidence he would use in his essay. It read, "Race still matters in many corners of our society, and some people can't get past it. But in education, it is changing for the better. The problem is, it may be changing too slowly." Doug finished his guided instruction with David by focusing on the metacognitive. "Take a look at your planning sheet," he asked. "Are there any gaps?" When David replied that there weren't, Doug continued, "Think about what you know about your teacher's expectations. Will this meet his criteria?" David replied in the affirmative. "How do you know this? What's your evidence?" Doug asked. He and David discussed the English teacher's past feedback on David's essays, and based on this discussion made a few more adjustments to his planning sheet. "Ready to go?" Doug asked. David grinned: "Ready."

Defining Prompts

Prompts are statements made by the teacher to focus students on the cognitive and metacognitive processes needed to complete a learning task. They may be phrased in the form of a question, such as when Doug asked David, "Is your reader going to understand your position based on the thesis you've written?" In other cases, they are delivered as a declarative statement, like when Doug said, "We need to transfer these ideas to the planning sheet your teacher gave you. That will give you an idea of where the holes are in your essay." Cues, as we'll see in the next chapter, can be integrated with prompts, as when Doug drew a table on a sheet of paper to use as a tool for visually organizing the essay.

Prompts differ from the questioning techniques discussed in Chapter 2 based on intent. Questions delivered to determine what a student knows and doesn't know provide the teacher with an initial measure of what should occur next. The intent is to informally gauge where the student is in order to plan subsequent instructional moves, including prompts. Prompting represents the next step that occurs in guided instruction and is focused on getting the student to do the cognitive and metacognitive work required to complete the task. Questioning is about *assessment*; prompting is about *doing*.

Prompts fall into two broad categories: cognitive and metacognitive. A cognitive prompt is intended to trigger academic knowledge, especially the factual and procedural information needed to complete the task. Cognition is about thinking, and a cognitive prompt focuses on the reasoning necessary to process information and apply it. Cognition occurs in the brain. The field of neurobiology has focused on the process that humans use to think and understand. In general, humans "think" in their cortex, the outer surface of the brain, or the part you see when looking at a postmortem brain. However, although we all use the same general structures, we don't all "think" in the same place. The connectivity inside the cortex varies widely across individuals, which makes studying thinking very difficult. An interesting implication from neurobiological evidence is important to our discussion of cognition: the thinking system is not innate, as it is not dictated in specific genes. What is innate is a learning system, and we all have learning systems ready to be activated. We categorize cognitive prompts as those that activate background knowledge and those that encourage students to apply this knowledge to complete a process or procedure.

Other prompts are metacognitive in nature. If cognition is about thinking, then metacognition is thinking about thinking. In their book *How People Learn* (Bransford, Brown, & Cocking, 1999), the authors define metacognition as "people's abilities to predict their performances on various tasks ... and to monitor their current levels of mastery and understanding" (p. 12). They further advise that teaching practices focused on metacognition include "sense-making, self-assessment, and reflection on what worked and what needs improving" (p. 12). Metacognitive prompts require students to consider ways to problem solve (heuristics) and to reflect upon their learning.

In the next section, we discuss these four types of prompts—background knowledge, process or procedure, heuristic, and reflective—in more detail. Our goal is not to artificially parse the language of teachers in guided instruction, but instead to consider the relationship between the teacher's intent and the learner's ability to use the prompt to do the heavy cognitive and metacognitive lifting required as they assume more responsibility and gain conceptual understanding.

Prompting for Background Knowledge

What learners already know about a given topic is probably the best predictor of their understanding. In other words, the absence of background knowledge interferes with understanding. Of course, a highly motivated learner can compensate for some missing background knowledge, but even an exceptionally motivated learner will not achieve at the highest levels when background knowledge is missing.

Consider Brian's situation. He wants to learn, as he says, "everything there is to know about digital photography." Even though he doesn't have a lot of experience, Brian wants to learn how to take excellent pictures with his new digital camera. He's very motivated and hangs around the school technology coordinator. But when he reads something related to photography, he's often confused. For example, while reading a book he found in the library, Brian comes across the following sentence: "Unless a scene includes important elements in shade, it's worth underexposing slightly by setting a minus exposure compensation factor, –0.5 perhaps" (Burian, 2004, p. 120). Just consider the background knowledge that is assumed in that single sentence. The individual words aren't that hard to read, but what they mean in this context matters.

Let's take our analysis of this sentence a little further. Brian probably knows by now what a *scene* is, and how that applies to photography. But *element* throws him. The last time he heard someone use the term *element* he was in science, specifically chemistry. So he's got to be thinking, "What do the elements have to do with shade?" He might even ask himself, "Are there important elements in shade? Oxygen, of course. What else?" Not knowing what the author means, Brian focuses on the remainder of the sentence. *Underexposing* comes next, but he's not sure what that means or how to do it. He makes a mental note to look up underexposing on the Internet. Then comes the phrase *minus exposure compensation factor*. Brian knows minus: to subtract. He knows that exposure has to do with the lens opening. So he's thinking that he has to subtract something from the lens opening. It's compensating for something. It's some factor that must be important. Brian is on the verge of understanding but gives up and closes the book.

Even highly motivated students fail to understand when they do not have—or do not activate—the relevant background knowledge. Unfortunately, background knowledge is often neglected in classrooms. Instead, teachers tend to focus on instruction based on comprehension strategies, using terms such as *predicting, summarizing, inferring, visualizing, monitoring*, and *questioning*. But you have to ask yourself, which of these would have helped Brian make sense of the text that he desperately wanted to read? What would a reasonable prediction for that text be? How might he infer, or read between the lines? What does he see in his mind, other than shade and himself trying to take a picture? Simply said, comprehension-strategy instruction *does not work* in the absence of background knowledge.

So what we do we mean by *background knowledge*? In reality, background knowledge is influenced by what you have been formally taught (also known as prior knowledge) and what you have experienced personally. So prior knowledge can be generally assumed to be constant across a group of students. The vast majority of students who complete 4th grade in California have been taught about the Gold Rush and the California missions. And the vast majority of students who have taken Earth science understand the role that tectonic plates play in earthquakes and volcanoes. That's not to say that some students didn't learn it well or that some forgot it, but their prior knowledge includes that information, and it's fairly predictable. Far less predictable is the background knowledge individual students have because of their lived experiences. We worked at an elementary school in which every student in grades 3 through 5 spent several weeks—yes, *weeks*—in museums each school year. The background knowledge they developed included their experiences with the San Diego Zoo, the Museum of Man, the Natural History Museum, the Museum of Photographic Arts, and many others. Imagine the complexity of their background knowledge by the time they got to middle school and how different it would be from students who did not have those experiences and who might be sitting in the same 6th grade class. That's the reality of classrooms today; student diversity extends to background knowledge.

Marzano (2004) notes that there are two ways to build background knowledge: directly and indirectly. Direct approaches are those that allow learners to experience the world around them, much like our students and their museum experiences. But direct experiences are not always practical. They're often expensive and require travel, and sometimes they're just impossible. Until time travel is perfected, students can't directly experience the building of the pyramids of the pharaohs. So for most topics we use indirect approaches, including reading. Reading is one of the more effective indirect ways for building students' background knowledge. We believe that teachers should encourage their students to read widely on the topics they're studying.

But there's another way to build students' background knowledge that more directly involves the teacher. Through our prompting, we can say or do the just-right thing to build the student's background knowledge while we ensure that the student engages in cognitive work.

Consider the moves Mr. Jackson makes as he builds students' background knowledge through prompting. The class is focused on the digestive system. Students are working in groups to create a game (*ala Jeopardy!* or *Who Wants to Be a Millionaire?*) that will review the content they've learned. Mr. Jackson is meeting with four students who have not yet demonstrated their understanding of the content. Mauricio has missed several days of school due to an illness and has been attending all of the guided instruction groups to catch up. The other three students in the group struggle with learning for a variety of reasons. Mr. Jackson has a text for them to review; he starts with the illustrations and headings. He has selected specific sentences from the text that serve as key ideas that his students should know, the first of which is this: "When you eat foods—such as bread, meat, and vegetables—they are not in a form that the body can use as nourishment."

Mr. Jackson starts the conversation by asking Mauricio to retell what this sentence means.

Mauricio: So I think it says that your body can't use meat like it is meat. It has to be changed.

Jessica: But that's what we eat to live. That's good eating.

Russell: I don't eat any vegetables. I only like the meat and bread from this, like a hamburger.

Mr. Jackson: How does that meat change so that your body can use it? Russell?

Russell: It doesn't change. It's meat.

Mr. Jackson: So let's think about what we know about nourishment and our food. There's a process that it goes through, right? [They nod in agreement.] What's the first step? You know this because you do it several times a day.

Sarah: The first thing to eat? Is that what you mean?

Mr. Jackson: Yeah, the first thing.

Sarah: You take a bite.

Mr. Jackson: Exactly, right on. So you've changed the food, right?

Russell: Yeah, but it's still meat.

Mr. Jackson: It sure is. But it's changed a bit, and will change more. Remember we talked about different kinds of changes. Physical, chemical . . .

Russell: So the first thing, when you bite it, it's a physical change, right?

Mr. Jackson: You know it! And then what happens?

As Mr. Jackson continues his guided instruction, it becomes apparent that within a very short time, his prompts have helped students develop the background knowledge they need to catch up with their peers.

But not all knowledge is equally relevant at a given moment. Having a pet snake might be interesting, but it isn't really relevant to learning the fable "The Snake and the Farmer." Nor is experience living on a farm, for that matter. The fable is about putting aside thoughts of hatred and revenge when visual reminders are present. In other words, it's not really about a snake or a farmer, and activating that background knowledge won't improve understanding.

We've attempted to develop a system to determine "core" versus "incidental" background knowledge. Our system contains the following four indicators to determine the relevance or worthiness of the specific background knowledge (Fisher & Frey, 2009a):

• **Representation**—If the information is foundational to understanding the main concepts, it's probably core background knowledge. If the information is interesting but peripheral to the main concepts, it's probably incidental background knowledge.

• **Transmission**—If the information requires multiple exposures and experiences, it's probably core background knowledge. Alternatively, if it can be explained or defined easily (using a label, fact, or name), it's probably incidental background knowledge.

• **Transferability**—If the information will be needed again to understand future concepts, it's probably core background knowledge. But if it's specific to this concept and unlikely to be used in the future, it's probably incidental background knowledge.

• **Enduring**—If the idea will likely be remembered after details are forgotten, it's probably core background knowledge. Conversely, when ideas, details, and specifics are not likely to be recalled later, it's probably incidental background knowledge.

Determining which is core background knowledge, worthy of attention during guided instruction, and which is not is an important part of guided instruction. Understanding the difference ensures that the teacher has a plan for developing or activating students' background knowledge.

In the digestive system example, Mr. Jackson was activating students' background knowledge. They had the information, but they didn't use it to make sense of the task at hand. In other situations, the teacher will need to develop students' background knowledge. Consider the following example, in which Ms. Branson is reading *Night* (Wiesel, 2006) to her class. She determined that among the core background knowledge her students needed so they could understand the text were concepts of the Holocaust, imprisonment, and persecution—specifically religious persecution. Some of the topics she considered incidental to understanding the book included Hitler, concentration camps, and the genre of memoir. Ms. Branson knows that the incidental background knowledge topics are not unimportant, but rather are not critical to understanding the text they are reading. As a check of their core background knowledge, Ms. Branson has her students do a three-minute quick-write about the Holocaust before starting to read the first chapter. She reads over several students' shoulders to assess their understanding of this concept. In addition, she collects the papers and reviews them while students are working on their vocabulary study following her read-aloud. She is reassured that her students understand this historical event (after all, it was the focus of their first-semester history course) and that she does not need to focus her instructional time on this aspect of their background knowledge. She also knows that she'll want to activate this background knowledge periodically to ensure that her students grasp the meanings in the book and place them in historical context.

Later, she asks students to create a visual image of the term *imprisonment*. They start this assignment at school and are asked to finish it at home. The following day Ms. Branson collects the images before reading on in the book. Looking at the images her students created informs her that she needs to build their background knowledge. Some of the students seem to understand the confines of prison, but others drew crimes being committed or scenes of executions. After the reading for the day, Ms. Branson begins a conversation with her students about the concept of imprisonment:

Ms. Branson: I see inside this word *imprisonment* the word *prison.* The word doesn't tell me why a person is in prison, but that the person is, in fact, in prison. I'm interested in your ideas about prison—not why people get into prison, but what it's like in prison. Let's start with the physical characteristics of prison. I'd like you to write three physical characteristics of prisons on your paper. When you have three, please stand up. [Students start writing, and Ms. Branson talks with individual students as they do so. They take a few minutes to complete the task. When they are standing, Ms. Branson resumes.]

Ms. Branson: You all remember the whip-around. You say one thing from your list, and you listen to the things others say. If you have the same item on your list, check it off. We only hear new ideas, so once it's been said you don't have to say it. When all three items from your list have been said, by you or anyone else, you can sit down. This will get a bunch of ideas out in the air for us to talk about.

Students, one at a time: Small, cold, stone, bars, dirty, bad food, smells rotten, peeling paint, junky mattress.... [The list continues until all students are seated.]

Ms. Branson: What a descriptive list of the physical conditions of imprisonment we have! Now let's think about the psychological characteristics. Let's make another list of three items to describe the psychological characteristics of imprisonment.

The conversation continues as Ms. Branson develops the core background knowledge her students will need to fully understand the text she is reading to them. Through her prompting, she has ensured that her students engage in cognitive work. The result is increased understanding and improved achievement. But even more important, Ms. Branson and Mr. Jackson are building their students' confidence and competence. Their effort improves the learning environment, as we all know that when we feel good about what we're doing and we think we can accomplish the tasks at hand, we're simply happier and more likely to engage.

Prompting for Process or Procedural Knowledge

Another reason to prompt students involves helping them complete a process or procedure. Of course, this works when there is a process or procedure to complete, and not everything we learn fits into this category. Some things that students need to learn are *declarative*, meaning that they involve labels, names, facts, and lists. In other words, declarative knowledge is factual knowledge (Anderson, 1976). There are essentially two types of declarative knowledge:

• **Episodic knowledge**—Memory for events or "episodes" (i.e., where, when, who with, and so on) that are usually associated with autobiographical references.

• **Semantic knowledge**—Memory for long-established knowledge about objects, facts, and word meanings.

Declarative knowledge is assessed in checking for understanding and is often the focus of guided instruction because it relates to background knowledge and direct explanations and modeling. The other type of knowledge, procedural knowledge, involves not the "what" but rather the "how." It's the knowledge required to perform a specific task. That's the type of knowledge we're working on in this section: knowledge about how to do something.

In reality, most of the time we operate within and between these two types of knowledge. Take driving a car, for example. You have to know which is the gas pedal and which is the brake (*declarative*), *and* you have to know how to use them (*procedural*). You have to know which device is the turn signal, which operates the windshield wipers, and which is the gear shifter, *and* you have to know how to use them. If you've ever attempted to teach someone to drive, perhaps a teenager in your own household, you know that focusing only on declarative knowledge will not result in an ability to perform the task.

Task Analysis

One of the first steps for guiding students in procedural knowledge involves completing a task analysis (Kirwan & Ainsworth, 1992). We use procedures to ride a bike, for long division, in our writing, to diagnose diseases, and for a host of other things. Procedures are important in our lives because they help us negotiate situations. Procedures can be cognitive or psychomotor or both. Procedures that are cognitive in nature are called *rules*, according to Gagne's (1985) theory of learning, whereas procedures involving motor skills are called *executive routines*. Of course, procedures vary in complexity, and some involve decision points called branching points. Consider the procedural knowledge involved in reading. There are a number of rules that must be used, as well as a number of branching points based on what the author has done. When students struggle, we can analyze the procedure that has broken down, develop a task analysis, and prompt them to higher levels of understanding.

Various task analyses are available on the Internet, but they're easy enough to create. As Jonassen, Tessmer, and Hannum (1999) note, a task analysis "is a process of analyzing and articulating the kind of learning that you expect the learners to know how to perform" (p. 3). They recommend that a task analysis be developed for a variety of reasons, including to—

- determine the instructional goals and objectives;
- define and describe in detail the tasks and sub-tasks that the student will perform;
- specify the knowledge type (declarative, structural, and procedural knowledge) that characterizes a job or task;
- select learning outcomes that are appropriate for instructional development;
- prioritize and sequence tasks;
- determine instructional activities and strategies that foster learning;
- select appropriate media and learning environments; and
- construct performance assessments and evaluation. (p. 3)

The process of developing a task analysis consists of five distinct steps (Jonassen et al., 1999):

1. Classifying tasks according to learning outcomes.
2. Inventorying tasks—identifying tasks or generating a list of tasks.
3. Selecting tasks—prioritizing tasks and choosing those that are more feasible and appropriate if there are a number of different tasks that require instruction.

4. Decomposing tasks—identifying and describing the components of the tasks, goals, or objectives.

5. Sequencing tasks and sub-tasks—defining the sequence in which instruction should occur that will best facilitate learning.

Sometimes the task analysis is fairly simple. Consider, for example, the steps involved in being ready to learn in math class. An analysis of this part of the learning might include the following steps:

1. Enter the room and find the correct desk.
2. Clear desk of unnecessary items.
3. Place unnecessary items under the chair.
4. Place your math book, paper, a pencil, and your calculator on your desk.
5. Look to the board for the "do now" problem and begin work.

Of course, other tasks require a much longer analysis. Consider the task analysis for teaching students the order of operations. They probably already have some background knowledge, specifically prior knowledge. They typically can recite "Please excuse my dear Aunt Sally." They might even know what each of the letters in the mnemonic means (parenthesis, exponents, multiplication, division, addition, subtraction). But when they get stuck, what prompting will help? Using a task analysis will ensure that the prompts provided to the learner are provided just in time, and not on components of the task the learner already understands.

There are four rules for the order of operations:

1. Simplify all operations inside parentheses.
2. Simplify all exponents, working from left to right.
3. Perform all multiplications and divisions, working from left to right.
4. Perform all additions and subtractions, working from left to right.

It might be enough to use a task analysis of the four rules, but it might not be. You might have to analyze each rule, breaking it down into its component steps in the process. Parenthetically, when you take the time to break down the procedure or process into a task analysis, you really do know what you need to teach, and you can more easily anticipate the errors students may make and the misconceptions they may have.

A sample form for creating and administering a task analysis appears in Figure 3.1. This tool includes a key for the type of prompts and cues that were used for the student to complete the task on various dates. A careful analysis of the prompt and cues used over time can help the teacher fade them, as we need to be careful not to create dependent learners. For example, if one step on the task analysis focused on word-solving strategies during reading, over time the teacher could monitor the types of prompts and cues that were used to ensure that the student completed that step. An analysis of the task over time would reveal progress or a need to focus additional instruction on that step.

Chaining

Once the procedure is clear, chaining is an effective way to prompt students. There are two ways to chain prompts: backward and forward. In forward chaining, you start with the first step in the process or procedure and work through to the end. The key to forward chaining is the role of the teacher. When the student cannot respond to further prompting to accomplish the task, the teacher assumes responsibility and completes the procedure.

For example, consider the student who is stuck on a word problem in mathematics. Using forward chaining, the teacher prompts the student to start with the first step, which is probably to read the problem. The student completes this step. The second step might be to associate numbers with the known variables. Let's listen in as Ms. Wells engages in guided instruction with a group of students who are stuck on the following word problem: "It takes 6 cubes to build a staircase with 3 steps. How many cubes will be needed for 11 steps?"

Ms. Wells: You've read the problem, so what's next?

Arturo: Figure out the numbers for the variables we know.

Meeta: We know 6, 3, and 11. But that doesn't help me.

Ms. Wells: But let's just take some notes and connect the numbers with what they represent in this problem. The 6 represents something.

Figure 3.1 | **Task Analysis Data Collection Tool**

Student Name: _____ Grade: _____

Instructional Task:

_____

_____

Student Performance:

_____

KEY: I = Independently   B = Background   H = Heuristic

            V = Verbal/signed cue   M = Model or Explanation   R = Reflective

            P = Physical cue

Task Analysis Steps	Dates				
1.					
2.					
3.					
4.					
5.					
6.					
7.					
8.					
9.					
10.					

Notes:

Meeta: Cubes.

Ms. Wells: Yes, exactly. For how many steps?

Arturo: Three.

Ms. Wells: Let's label this so we can use the information in the next step. And the 11?

Meeta: How many steps we want to have.

Ms. Wells: Perfect. Is that it? Do we have any other numbers to associate with known variables?

Meeta: Nope. Then we gotta figure out the formulas or equations.

Ms. Wells: Yes. Do you have it from here?

Arturo: I think so, but just wait for a minute to see.

Ms. Wells: I'll be right here.

Arturo and Meeta set up the problem and correctly answer it using the procedures they know well, including looking at key words or phrases such as *is*, *of*, *by*, or *together with*; identifying a starting point; substituting known amounts into the equation; and solving for the answer. They knew part of the procedure, but not how to start. Forward chaining provided the prompting they needed to be successful. And more important, it provided their teacher with information about what her students are doing well and where they still need instruction.

Backward chaining is the opposite of forward chaining. In backward chaining, the teacher does all of the upfront work and the student completes the final step (and experiences immediate success). As the student integrates the procedures into his habits, the teacher stops earlier and earlier, allowing the student to complete more and more of the task independently. Every parent has done this with a child; it's good teaching. In the classroom, backward chaining can be used when students are introduced to new and complex ideas or when students struggle with grade-level lessons.

Mr. Zanella uses backward chaining in his biology class as part of his instruction. For example, during a sea star dissection lab, Mr. Zanella conducted all of the prep work and most of the dissection, talking aloud about the process and letting the students see what was happening through the document camera. Near the end of the dissection, he turned the lab over to students to finish the tasks and complete the report. In doing so, he ensured their success and sensitized them to lab procedures. Over the next several dissections, he did less and less of the work, releasing responsibility to his students earlier and earlier in the process. As one of his students said, "I didn't think I could do it, but now I know that dissections are how we learn about anatomy and physiology. I'm way proud of my sheep brain dissection. I really got to see, up close, the structures we've been learning about in class. I don't think I could have done it all the first time, with the sea star, but now I can."

Models, Templates, and Frames

One of the ways to prompt students to complete a task involves the strategic use of models, templates, and frames. In essence, these are scaffolds, typically in written form, that provide the student with the support necessary to be successful with academic English. Academic English requires attention to a specific set of rules and procedures, some of which are breakable. Models, templates, and frames—like all scaffolds—are designed to be removed once the procedure or process has been learned. They aren't meant to be permanent, any more than you'd like to live in a condo complex with scaffolds outside your window for the rest of your life.

In our study of struggling writers (Fisher & Frey, 2003) we found that the use of writing models such as mentor texts and sentence and paragraph frames provided students with the support they needed to write increasingly sophisticated compositions. College composition experts Gerald Graff and Cathy Birkenstein (2006) recommend the use of frames (they call them templates) as an effective way for developing students' academic writing skills. They defend the use of frames or templates by noting the following:

> After all, even the most creative forms of expression depend on established patterns and structures. Most songwriters, for instance, rely on a time-honored verse-chorus-verse pattern, and few people would call Shakespeare uncreative because he didn't invent the sonnet or dramatic forms that he used to such dazzling effect.... Ultimately, then, creativity and originality lie not in the avoidance of established forms, but in the imaginative use of them. (pp. 10–11)

As Graff and Birkenstein correctly note, writing frames help students incorporate established norms of academic writing, whether that calls for summarizing information in social studies, completing a lab report, or writing a persuasive letter.

To build the oral language skills of students in the Chula Vista Elementary School District, a team of teachers met to develop language frames that students across the district could use while speaking. These teachers understand that oral practice with academic English apprentices students into academic writing and reading because it supports the process and procedures required of the language. The list is pages and pages long, but here are a few examples of the frames used to guide students in English language arts:

- I can predict that _____ because _____.
- The setting of the story is _____ and is important because

    _____.

- I believe that _____ will happen because _____.
- The main idea is _____; the facts and details that support it are _____.
- In the beginning, _____ (character) was _____ (feelings/ traits) because _____ (evidence).
- The passage _____ is mostly about _____. One important detail is _____.
- I think that _____ would symbolize the character well because it represents _____.
- I agree with _____ because _____.
- I think _____ might change the outcome of the story if _____.
- In the story _____ by _____, the author's purpose is to teach us that/to _____.
- Some people might believe that _____, but I believe _____.

Just imagine the conversations students have about what they're reading because they have the support they need to share their thinking. As a quick example, here's what we overhead when some 4th grade students who are English language learners were talking about the book they both had been reading, *Shiloh* (Naylor, 1991):

Raquel: Some people might believe that Marty was wrong, but I believe that he did the right thing to save Shiloh.

Martha: I agree with you because Shiloh was abused. I can predict that Marty will get to keep Shiloh because he is hiding him from Judd.

Raquel: I believe that some bad things will happen because Marty has to hide and not tell his mom the truth.

Language frames and mentor texts aren't limited to use in oral language development. Consider the frames that Ms. Anderson and Ms. Smith provided to their students to guide their completion of an essay for English (see Figure 3.2). The students were working on a complex essential question: Does age matter? Their teachers wanted to be sure that the students had the best support possible to be successful. They also knew that students vary the frames when they become comfortable with them. They had experience with students trying out the frames and then incorporating them into their habits. Naturally, they also interacted with their students and provided prompts in other ways, in addition to the language frames.

Similarly, Ms. Denton wanted to ensure that her students wrote summaries of the content they were learning in their middle school science class. She provided them with a frame to use as a support for the process of summarizing informational texts. Here's how she used the frame to summarize an article she read related to the world's water supply:

> The main idea of this passage is that fresh water is scarce. One example that supports this main idea is that people do not have clean drinking water in parts of Africa. Another example that supports this main point is Southern California is buying water from other states and will run out. In addition, some of the water supply is contaminated because of runoff from industrial plants. Finally, the data that the author provides in the chart illustrate that we are running out of fresh water in the world.

In each of the examples presented, the language frames provide students with prompts about a process or procedure to complete that relate to academic English. They don't simply provide students an answer, but rather facilitate

Figure 3.2 | Possible Language Frames for "Does Age Matter?" Essay

My own view is that _____. Although I concede that _____, I still maintain that _____. For example, _____. Although some might object that _____, I reply that _____. The issue is important because _____.

Introducing Standard Views
Common sense seems to dictate that _____.
It is often said that _____.
My whole life I have heard it said that _____.
You would think that _____.
Many people assume that _____.
I've always believed that _____.
Although I should know better by now, I cannot help thinking that _____.
At the same time that I believe _____, I also believe _____.

Disagreeing with Reasons
By focusing on _____, X overlooks the deeper problem of _____.
I think that X is mistaken because she/he overlooks _____.
X's claim that _____ rests upon the questionable assumption that _____.
My own view, however, is that _____.

Agreeing
I agree that _____ because my experience _____ confirms it.
I agree that _____, a point that needs emphasizing since so many people believe that _____.
Although I concede that _____, I still insist that _____.
I'm of two minds about X's claim that _____. On the one hand, I agree that _____. On the other hand, I'm not sure if _____.
X is right that _____.
The evidence shows that _____.
Anyone familiar with _____ should agree that _____.

Entertaining Objections
Yet some readers may challenge my view that _____. After all, many believe that _____. Indeed, my own argument that _____ seems to ignore _____ and _____.
Yet is it always true that _____? Is it always the case, as I have been suggesting, that _____?

Figure 3.2 | **Possible Language Frames for "Does Age Matter?" Essay (*cont.*)**

Conclusion

My point here—that _____—should interest those who _____. Beyond this limited audience, however, my point should speak to anyone who cares about the larger issue of _____.

Paragraph Starters/Transitions

Chapter _____ explores _____, while Chapter _____ examines _____.

Having just argued that _____, let us now turn our attention to _____.

Consider _____, for example.

To take a case in point, _____.

Even more important, _____.

But above all, _____.

Incidentally, _____.

---

their performance and demonstration of content understanding. As such, models, templates, and frames are an appropriate scaffold for student learning because they provide students with prompting related to the process and procedures necessary for academic writing.

Prompting for Heuristic Knowledge

As described in Chapter 2, heuristics are the techniques we use to solve a problem. Much of our heuristic knowledge is built through experience with a problem, and we learn over time what works best for us. For instance, Nancy finds that a useful heuristic is to keep meeting notes in a single notebook so she can access them anytime she needs them. Doug makes cryptic to-do lists on a small pad of paper he keeps in his car. But academic heuristics don't have to rely on a trial-and-error approach. They can be fostered during guided instruction using prompts that encourage students to apply their judgment, draw on previous experiences, and use academic knowledge to solve problems.

Heuristic knowledge differs from processes and procedures in that the problems the learners confront are ill-defined when compared to clear-cut tasks such as outlining an essay or adding decimals. The heuristics learners acquire through academic tasks are less formal, but are no less important than the processes and procedures students use. Examples of heuristics include the following:

- Drawing a visual representation of a word problem in mathematics
- Considering the advantages and disadvantages of a political decision in history
- Retracing one's use of a lab procedure in science to figure out why an experiment did not work
- Weighing the relative merits of four book choices in English

Much of our heuristic knowledge is developed as we confront problems that are challenging but not impossible. This quality—"challenging but not impossible"—is a central tenet of the Gradual Release of Responsibility model. The goal is to design tasks that stretch students a bit without overwhelming them. Most of us have experienced the tipping point in our own classrooms, as we have seen what occurs when we cognitively overload a learner, who then begins to focus on his own inadequacy, the irrelevancy of the task, or the personal character of the teacher. The hood goes up, the head goes down, and a learning opportunity is lost.

However, guided instruction affords us with an ideal time to present a challenging task while still offering the scaffolds needed to accomplish it. In particular, the heuristic prompting we offer assists students in consolidating experiential and academic knowledge to address a problem. For this reason we have come to believe that errorless learning is not appropriate during guided instruction because it doesn't provide students with the chance to figure out what went wrong and then try a different approach.

Alternatively, the concept of productive failure (Kapur, 2008), although appropriate during collaborative learning with peers, may occur too early in the instructional cycle if students have not received instruction that builds heuristic knowledge. During productive failure, students work on a difficult task that may not result in accomplishment the first time around. However, the task is structured so that they have time to analyze their failure for possible errors and attempt it again. What's critical to productive failure is the ability to apply background knowledge, as well as procedural and heuristic knowledge, to come to a solution. But the assumption here is that students have that knowledge.

During guided instruction, we prefer productive success (Hung, Chen, & Lim, 2009). In a productive-success mode, the learner receives some scaffolded support in the form of "reinforcement of guiding tenets," especially in "resolving confusions" to achieve what the researchers call the eureka moment (p. 16). The kindergarten teacher who asks the young reader, "Does that sound right?" or "Does that make sense?" when the child makes an error is prompting her to resolve a confusion using a useful heuristic. When Doug reminded David in the opening scenario that he still had gaps in his essay plan, he was using a heuristic prompt that would hopefully result in David's later application of it when writing independently. Figures 3.3 and 3.4 present examples of heuristic prompts for early readers and older readers, respectively.

Examples of heuristic prompts abound in the classroom. One well-known heuristic is using the scientific method to determine if an experiment is coherent. The development of the scientific method is in part a product of heuristic knowledge itself. Muslim scholars of the Middle Ages analyzed ancient Greek scientific experiments that drew faulty conclusions and speculated on possible errors that led those scientists astray. These speculations, as well as similar analyses in other parts of the world, led over time to more rigorous practices related to inquiry, investigation, and the use of inductive and deductive logic in experimental design. The scientific method, with its now familiar principles— observe, question, hypothesize, test, and draw conclusions—is meant to be more than a linear procedure to follow. It is intended to foster reasoning and problem solving at each stage of an experiment, from conception and design to data gathering and analysis.

Gita Patel has introduced the scientific method to her 7th grade science students in previous lessons and is ready for them to begin using it as a means for analyzing the design of experiments. She knows that she must develop this type

				General Problem Solving
Graphophonics	**Syntax**	**Semantics**	**Pragmatics**	
• Does it look right? • Cover the _____ to make the sound. • Does that word look like another word you know? • Did you see that word before on this page?	• Does it sound right? • Can you change the words so it will sound right? • How would you say it? • Make it sound like talking.	• Does it make sense? • Is that the word you expected to see there? • What do you expect to happen next in the story? Check to see if you're right. • Is there another word that would fit there and still make sense?	• Does that seem true to you? • Think about what you already know about _____. • Think about who is talking in the story. • Would _____ do (or say) that?	• Where is the tricky part? • Were you right? • How can you fix that? • What can you do to help yourself?

Figure 3.3 | **Heuristic Prompts for Early Readers**

of knowledge in order for them to design sound experiments for the school science fair; without experiences using the scientific method to solve problems, the concept will be of limited use.

Ms. Patel begins the lesson by reviewing the elements of the scientific method and then tells her students she's going to describe an experiment to them. She explains that she has two pairs of running shoes and wanted to know which pair would help her run faster. So she put on the first pair of shoes and timed herself for a mile. She ran it in 8 minutes, 50 seconds. She then put on the second pair of shoes and ran the same distance, this time in 9 minutes, 5 seconds. "I concluded that the first pair of shoes would help me run faster than the second. Am I right?" she asked.

Figure 3.4	**Heuristic Prompts for Older Readers**	
Before the Reading	**During the Reading**	**After the Reading**
• Based on this title, what do you expect this book will be about? • Have you read other books by this author? What do you expect? • What do you already know about _____ before you begin reading? • When you read the reviews on the back cover, did they change your expectations?	• What do you know about _____ so far? • What do you expect will happen next? • What has happened so far? Take a look in the text for clues. • Have you experienced something like this?	• What surprised you? Was that what the author wanted? • Does this remind you of any other books you've read? • If a person wanted to know more about this subject, where could he or she look? • Who would you recommend this to?

After directing the children to discuss the question with their science partners, she asks them for their responses. Noting that most accept her faulty conclusion, she prompts them by saying, "The scientific method can help you to decide if I'm right or not. Think about each step of my experiment." The partners go back to work, this time with a reminder to consider the scientific method. "Sometimes it helps to list the steps," she prompts as she listens in on the conversations occurring in the classroom.

Colleen and Rosa are deep in conversation. Colleen is making a list while Rosa is talking. "I think the question is good. Put a star next to 'question,'" she tells her partner. Ms. Patel prompts, "The next step is the hypothesis. Think about my hypothesis." The girls look at one another for a few moments, deep in thought. "Think about the logic that I'm using in my hypothesis," Ms. Patel adds. Colleen answers slowly, "Well … I'm not sure that shoes can make anyone run faster." Ms. Patel's face brightens. "I think you're onto something. What else doesn't seem right?" she asks. Now Rosa is eager to contribute: "There's no … what do you call it when you only do it once? Trials. There's no repeated trials." Ms. Patel now uses an elaboration question to find out more about what Rosa knows. "Can you tell me more about that?" she asks. Rosa replies, "You should have run like five times with each pair of shoes, and then you could average them." Colleen joins in, "And sometimes changed which pair of shoes you used first." Ms. Patel states, "So now you're analyzing the testing phase of my experiment. Keep going!" With that, Ms. Patel moves to listen to another set of partners, confident that Rosa and Colleen are using what they know about the scientific method to analyze for errors in experimental design.

Error analysis, as in the example on using the scientific method, is one way to encourage heuristic thinking. The other side of this problem-solving coin is error prevention. Teachers can foster productive success by providing prompts intended to help students avoid errors that are likely to interfere. When a teacher looks over the shoulder of a student and says, "Don't forget to indent when you begin the next paragraph," he is prompting for error prevention. When Nancy develops rubrics for an assignment, she includes a column titled "Errors to Avoid." The intent of error-prevention prompts isn't to create error-less learning, but instead to draw students' attention to the kinds of mistakes that are associated with the task. Knowing what *not* to do, as well as what to do, is essential to learning.

Fifth grade mathematics teacher Janet Carter is providing her students with guided instruction as they learn how to find the mean, median, mode, and range for a set of numbers. Ms. Carter lists a set of nine two-digit numbers on the whiteboard and asks her students to copy them down and solve for the four conditions. She prompts them for error prevention: "Always remember to order the data and cross off [the numbers] so you don't miss one." As students work out the problem, she looks closely at Jonah's work.

Ms. Carter: Can you tell me how you're beginning the problem?

Jonah: I copied the numbers off the board.

Ms. Carter: Hmm, I can see that. Look at the numbers you've written down and think about how that compares with the advice I just gave.

Jonah [looking at paper]: I should put them in order.

Ms. Carter: OK, do that, and then let's talk about another tricky part.

After Jonah recopies the numbers in ascending order, she prompts again:

> **Ms. Carter:** Tell me again the advice I gave.
>
> **Jonah:** Put them in order?
>
> **Ms. Carter:** And ...
>
> **Jonah:** Cross them off? As I use them?
>
> **Ms. Carter:** You've got it. I'll watch while you do the first one.

Ms. Carter recognized that merely giving a prompt is often not enough. Especially when it comes to heuristic prompts, it is useful to observe how students integrate the prompts into their learning. Some tasks are more easily observed than others, as when Jonah is solving the math problem. At other times, discussion about their learning is required, as when Ms. Patel talks with Colleen and Rosa about their use of the scientific method. Because heuristic prompts are metacognitive in nature, they are one way to foster awareness of how one learns. Another is using reflective prompts to encourage noticing.

Prompting for Reflective Knowledge

The prompts used for reflective learning are perhaps the most well-known, yet least understood, aspect of teaching. Effective teachers routinely ask students to contemplate what they have learned. Teachers of young students in particular encourage daily goal setting by their students and then provide them with time at the end of the day to reflect on how they did. First grade teacher Kevin O'Shea makes a point of checking in with Mitchell each day about his self-reflection. Mitchell writes two goals every morning and then rates his work for the day by choosing a happy, neutral, or sad face. Under the goal "I will try my best," Mitchell selected the neutral face.

> **Mr. O'Shea:** I see you chose this [pointing to paper] for your goal. Why did you choose that one?
>
> **Mitchell** shrugs his shoulders.
>
> **Mr. O'Shea:** Let's think about your day. What was the best thing you did today?

Mitchell: I read good at the reading table.

Mr. O'Shea: Yes, you did! I was really impressed. That must have made you happy.

Mitchell: Yeah, it did.

Mr. O'Shea: That would make it a happy face. But you didn't pick that. What was the least favorite thing you did today?

Mitchell [pauses]: I didn't do my math so good.

Mr. O'Shea: How do you know?

Mitchell: I got 4 wrong out of 10 problems.

Mr. O'Shea: That didn't feel good.

Mitchell: Nope.

Mr. O'Shea: But your goal says, "I will do my best," not "I will be the best." Were you trying?

Mitchell: I guess.

Mr. O'Shea: Tell me how you tried your best.

Mitchell: I checked my answers.

Mr. O'Shea: That doesn't sound like someone who doesn't care. That just sounds like someone who needs some more help with math. How about if we work on these again tomorrow?

Mitchell: OK. That would be good.

Mr. O'Shea: So what do you think about your goal now?

Young children need lots of opportunities to engage in reflective conversation because they are developmentally not fully ready to be metacognitive on their own. That's why simple goal-setting exercises are useful for primary students. By the time they reach the age of 8 or 9, they are engaging in more formal reflective thinking about their learning but still need many opportunities to develop this type of knowledge. One of the best ways to encourage reflective thinking is through interactive journal writing.

Interactive Journal Writing

As with other types of prompts, intent is important. Journals are kept for a variety of reasons, especially as a tool for summarizing, self-evaluating, and engaging in inquiry. You'll notice that we have chosen the word *interactive* to describe journal writing as a tool for prompting reflective thought on learning. An interactive journal is one that moves back and forth between the student and the teacher, sometimes with comments and further reflective prompts. The reflective writing prompts we use with students are general in nature, in the sense that they are not discipline specific. However, we return to these same prompts again and again precisely because we want to reinforce the utility of asking oneself questions like this on a routine basis:

- What did I learn today?
- What have I learned from reading this material?
- What don't I yet understand about this material?
- What do I think about this material?
- My goals for today were ...
- The most critical insight I gained was ...
- What I want to ask is ...
- How does this information make me feel?
- What am I pleased with?
- The best thing about today was ...
- The most surprising thing was ...
- I'd like to learn more about ...

Student responses to these reflective prompts are surprisingly insightful. Health educator Leanne Robertson relies on prompts like this because her 9th grade students are often reluctant to engage in conversation about sensitive issues related to emotional and sexual health matters. After a lesson on sexual abuse and violence, one student wrote this in response to the reflective prompt "How does this information make me feel?":

> I was 5 years old when it happened. I knew what happened right then and there so why didn't I say anything? I guess I thought it wasn't that big of a deal. I knew it couldn't be ok what he was doing to me, but I still let it happen. The incident that happened 11 years ago still pops into my head when I'm alone lying on my bed hugging my stuffed Cheshire cat. I knew it was wrong, I really did. I never said anything, not one word

EVER, until now. I have no idea why it affects me so much now instead of then.

The student then went on to disclose that she had been molested by a teenager at her after-school program when she was a kindergartner and had never told anyone until that day. Although this was not the response Ms. Robertson anticipated when she used this reflective prompt, she immediately set up a meeting with the student at which the girl could speak in private. In short order the parents and counselor were also involved, and the student received the support she needed to work through this difficult memory. Within months, and with the encouragement and support of her teacher and family, the student became involved in a charitable organization that provides support to other victims of sexual abuse. She wrote this in a later journal entry:

> What happened that day at school will be engraved in my mind forever. It's something I can't erase no matter how hard I try. I just have to keep filling the pages of my life with happy memories and replacing the bad with the good. There's a point in your life where you realize you have to stop blaming yourself and start sharing what you've kept bottled up because there's always someone out there who is willing to listen.

Fortunately, most reflective journal entries are not like this, but we include it here as a reminder that teaching is more than just academics. The guided instruction that we offer requires us to get close to students. The prompts that we provide for students can sometimes result in unexpected responses that challenge us to provide support psychologically as well as academically. This is also true when it comes to conferring, another reflective prompting technique that sometimes blends both personal and academic scaffolds.

Conferring

Conferring, or meeting with individual students, can be used as an independent learning task in which individual students meet with the teacher or other adult to discuss progress, ask questions, obtain feedback, and plan next steps for independent assignments. As you can see from this description, conferring also provides the teacher an opportunity to guide the student to reflective thinking. As we think about our own thinking, we review things that we'd like to do again as well as errors to avoid. Reflecting with a more knowledgeable other guides students to become increasingly metacognitive.

Conferring, as part of the Gradual Release of Responsibility model of instruction, occurs across subject areas. There is evidence of the effectiveness of conferring in reading, writing, mathematics, science, and more (Bomer, 1999; Heuser, 2000; Yeh, 2006). Although different experts identify different components that are necessary to conferring, the following are some general points worthy of note:

- **Let the learner lead.** In guided instruction, the learner sets the direction. Although the teacher can have a specific conferring point, such as discussing the process the student is using to solve math problems or giving feedback on an essay, it is the student who directs the course of the conversation. Letting the learner lead is important because students must learn to reflect on their learning when the teacher is not present.

- **Assume the learner has something to say.** Don't be deceived by outward signs of reluctance or by the age of the student. Most students recognize that one-to-one conversations are rare in busy classrooms, and they often warm to it after a few conversations. As part of guided instruction and prompting, we react to the learners, so getting them to talk is critical. Of course, the learners have to know that you're going to listen and that you care about what they have to say. Assuming the learner has something to say involves trust on both sides of the conversation.

- **Be patient and respect silence.** No one likes to be rushed in a conversation, and teachers are especially guilty of filling up the silences with their own voices. Give students time to compose their thoughts and to reflect. It is amazing how much more students will talk when their teachers remain quiet.

- **Look for the teachable moment.** Paying attention to what the student says—active listening—will reveal a number of teaching points. Although you may not be able to address the needs a student has during the conferring session, you can choose one to focus on as part of your prompting. The others can be recorded in your notes for future focus lessons or guided instruction. Remember that turning points in conversations often come near the end, not the beginning. These might be called "doorknob confessions" because they are usually a tossed-off remark as students are leaving the conversation ("Oh yeah, I'm kind of stuck on finding stuff on antibodies, but I'll work it out."). Don't get fooled into thinking that these remarks are inconsequential. Now's the time to invite the student to stay a bit longer while you provide a bit of instruction or guidance.

• **Keep it short.** We keep a timer on our tables to monitor the time—no more than five minutes. It's easy to get caught up in a sociable chat with an outgoing student, or to spend a very long time with a student who's got a laundry list of concerns. Schedule another conference for students with more support needs, and watch your time so you can get to all your students.

• **Include follow-up.** Each conferring session should include specific tasks that the student can complete before the next meeting. Before the student leaves, schedule the next conference. Doing so ensures that you always have a schedule prepared and notifies learners that you'll be inquiring about their progress at the next meeting. The follow-up can include other sessions, not one-to-one sessions, in which you use other prompts, cues, explanations, or modeling to ensure learning occurs.

Given these general points, think about what the learner is saying in the following excerpt from a conferring session in which Nancy was meeting with Marissa about her homework:

Marissa: So, I didn't do it, my homework.

Nancy: OK.

Marissa: So, like, it's too hard. I don't know where to start. My brain just hurts when I try to do it.

Nancy: I'm sorry to hear that. What is the next right thing we can do?

Marissa: I gotta learn this stuff 'cause I wanna pass the competency. But it's too hard. And plus, my mom makes me watch the kids and I don't have time.

Nancy: How about we try one now, just to see if it's too hard or if something else is getting in the way. That way you'll know what to do.

Marissa: OK, but they are hard. Do you know how to solve these 'quations? I started on this one, but then Anthony started screaming and I didn't want to get in trouble.

Nancy: You're not going to get in trouble here. Take it from where you left off.

Marissa: OK, so I already subtracted 4 from both sides. Now I need to divide by 3 on both sides. So, that's it? It's 12? The answer is 12?

Nancy: Looks like it. What does that tell you?

Marissa: I guess that one wasn't too hard. I better do the next one to be sure.

Nancy: Go for it.

Marissa [mumbling to herself as she completes the problem]: Yeah, I got this.

Nancy: So what did you learn about yourself?

Marissa: I'm letting others get me down. I think I'll go to office hours [tutorial] today and get them done so I'm not stressin' at home.

Nancy: So you have some confidence in yourself? Did you stop telling yourself you can't do this?

Marissa: Yeah, but I just needed to hear it again.

Summing Up

Prompts are an important element in the continuum of scaffolds used during guided instruction. They differ from the questioning discussed in Chapter 2 because of their intent. Whereas robust questioning is used to determine where a student is in order to plan the next instructional move, prompts are the move itself. Prompts can be cognitive or metacognitive. Examples of cognitive prompts include those that activate and build background knowledge, and those that support the use of a process or procedure. Background knowledge prompts focus on core concepts, which can be considered in light of their representation, transferability, transmission, and enduring qualities. Procedural prompts focus on the application of sequences or processes that result in the successful completion of an academic task. These procedures might be chained forward or backward to provide students with scaffolded support as they gain more cognitive control over a series of complex tasks.

Other prompts are metacognitive and are designed to encourage students to think about their thinking. The ability to problem solve is highly valued, and heuristic prompts remind students to consolidate their experiential and academic learning in order to approach novel problems. Reflective prompts provide students with opportunities to self-assess and contemplate their own learning. Reflective prompts sometimes can challenge us as educators because the relationship between self-concept and academic learning is intertwined. Together, these prompts provide students with the support they need to learn complex content.

4

Cueing Students' Attention for Learning

Kimberly Gans is about to let her 7th grade students in on a secret. She knows from experience that her social studies students often cling to a misconception that time somehow stops in other parts of the world when something of importance occurs in their history book. Not literally, of course, but nonetheless her students often assume that nothing else of interest occurred during the same time period they are examining. She finds this to be especially true when it comes to their study of world religions. "It's as if only one religion emerged at a time," she said. "The kids seem to have a hard time wrapping their heads around the idea that events could happen simultaneously."

She has taught them about the major religions, including Hinduism, Buddhism, Judaism, Christianity, and Islam, so the students have some background knowledge on the topic. But she also knows she is going to need to address this misconception directly if they are going to understand the multidimensional nature of history. Using a website graphic, she shows her students a 90-second applet of a world map showing the spread of religion over a period of 5,000 years (www.mapsofwar.com/ind/history-of-religion.html). She shows this several times so she can cue students to direct their attention to specific aspects of the map. "Notice how the colors on the map correspond to the time line that is developing on the bottom," she says. As she says this, she uses the laser pointer to highlight these two elements. After the students have viewed the map, she prepares to play it again, and this time she wants them to take a more active role: "When I show it next time, I want you to watch for the trigger points where conflict occurred. Think about what you know about the Crusades, for example." Efron and Mykia watch the applet again and discuss what they see while Ms. Gans listens in:

Efron: You can see the green [Islam] and the blue [Christianity] running into each other in that part that's sticking out.

Mykia: Spain. That's Spain.

Efron: Is that where there was fighting?

Mykia: Ms. Gans said to think about the Crusades.

Ms. Gans: Look in your book, on page 128.

Efron: Got it.

Ms. Gans: Now look at that chart at the bottom of the page [points].

Mykia [reading]: "The *Reconquista* was a series of wars between Spanish Christian kings and warring Muslim conquerors."

Ms. Gans: So tell me more about that.

After Mykia and Efron explain more about the Reconquista and the Crusades, Ms. Gans directs their attention again, this time moving her hand between Europe and Asia.

Ms. Gans: Now look at the video again and see what's happening at the same time in other parts of the world. In particular, look at what's occurring in Asia with Hinduism and Buddhism.

Over the next 10 minutes, Ms. Gans stops the video to fix her students' attention on simultaneous occurrences throughout the world. "The time line at the bottom really helps because it gives them dates to pay attention to as well. But there's lots of information packed into this 90 seconds. We have to watch it repeatedly if they're going to take it all in. I know what to look for, but they don't. I provide cues so I can help them focus on the details," says Ms. Gans.

Defining Cues

Cues are the means we use to shift learners' attention to a source of information that will increase their understanding, or to highlight an error or a misunderstanding. Cues draw on all modes of instruction and include visual, verbal, and intonation cues, as well as gestural, physical, and even environmental cues. They differ from prompts, which concentrate on cognitive and metacognitive processing, in that they are more direct and specific. Cues sometimes follow prompts, especially when the prompt has not been intense enough for the learner to locate a correct or complete response. When a teacher says, "When you connect the dots on the paper, think about the number that comes next," she is offering a procedural prompt. If the child veers from 2 to 7, she places her hand over the child's to steer her to 3 and says, "The number that comes after 2 is 3," thereby offering a physical cue and a verbal one at the same time. But you don't have to wait for a failed prompt to deliver a cue. Often the cue and the prompt are paired, as when a teacher refers to a graphic organizer while saying, "Think about what you know about the way an autobiography is organized. What do you expect to learn about Frederick Douglass by reading his autobiography?"

The emphasis with cueing is directing attention, and so a discussion of the role of attention in learning is warranted. Attention involves several parts of the brain and is governed by emotion as well as deliberate concentration. The emotional state of an organism is continually monitored by several structures, including the amygdalae, which are two almond-shaped neural clusters located in the midbrain. The amygdalae are involved in consolidation of memory, especially emotional memory. They are constantly on the lookout for rewards and threats, which is why emotional climate is so important to learning. A threatening situation, including a psychologically threatening one, often results in a shift in attention away from learning to threat response, sometimes called "fight or flight." The thalamus, which sits at the top of the brainstem near the center of the brain, is also important in attention. The thalamus sends nerve fibers out to the cerebral cortex in all directions and can be viewed as a pathway for determining what information should be let in and what may need to be blocked. This type of attention is sometimes referred to as "bottom up" because it is attuned to sensory and emotional input that is beyond conscious control.

Attention is also influenced by the executive function of the frontal lobes of the brain—the so-called "top-down" aspect of attention. This is where we make deliberate decisions, like "Pay attention to what she says, because the directions are important." The ability to make these decisions about concentration and focus matures with growth; young children are less able to sustain concentration than older ones for a host of biological, developmental, and social reasons. Attention is further influenced by motivation and interest; a learner can satiate on material so that it becomes boring and is no longer of interest.

Attention has spawned some myths, and these affect our teaching, not to mention our frustration level. One myth is that people can maintain a steady level of concentration for a long period. In truth, attention cycles quite often, and it's actually relatively difficult to sustain attention to one thing for a long time. In addition, it appears that the brain initiates downtime in order to process new information and strengthen neural networks, and that this is related to working (short-term) and long-term memory (Knudsen, 2007). Although opinions vary, the generally accepted range of sustained attention ranges from about 5 minutes for kindergarten students to about 20 minutes for adults. As we've been reminded since our own teacher preparation programs, learning activities need to be designed to offer opportunities to frequently shift attention and allow for processing time.

Another myth is the illusion of multitasking. In truth, the brain pays attention to one thing at a time. The shifts among attention networks can occur rapidly, but it is nearly impossible to sustain attention on two things at the same time, especially if those two things are competing with one another. This explains why cell phone laws that allow for hands-free devices have failed to have an effect on accident rates. If you're thinking that you can walk and chew gum at the same time, you're right, because these are motor behaviors rather than complex cognitive tasks that require attention. An example of competing attention is conducting a phone conversation while driving—two complex behaviors that each require lots of attention.

A third myth is that attentiveness is equally distributed among learners. In fact, the ability to attend to details is influenced by one's expertise. Two studies illustrate this point. The first is a comparison of expert and novice chess players. The experts were statistically significantly better able than average people to duplicate board configurations from real games, but performed the same as the novices on a similar task on board configurations of randomly placed pieces (Chase & Simon, 1973). In other words, the experts recognized complex configurations because they were possible and their experience told them so. The second study was performed with ballet and capoeira dancers. Both were shown video of dancers performing these two forms. Scans showed that the visual activity in their brains was more active when watching a dance they had trained in, compared to the one they had not trained in (Calvo-Merino, Glaser, Grezes, Passingham, & Haggard, 2005). One of the researchers in the study (Wellcome Trust, n.d.) said that he had been inspired by watching a broadcast of Olympic divers: "The commentator was saying 'and that was a double somersault with one and a half twists,' and I could barely see these movements" (paragraph 3).

Much like the expert commentator, you cue your audience (your students) to attend to important information they might otherwise overlook. In the next section of this chapter we discuss the types of cues used to help learners notice the information they need to gain knowledge. The cues you use in guided instruction provide them with the hints and clues students need to attend to relevant information.

Visual Cues

Visual cues are all around us. Just think about how many visual cues you use in a typical day: bold print, yellow lines in the street, or that round green sign suggesting a Starbucks is near. And the frequency of visual cues in our world is increasing exponentially because of the Internet. Gone are the flat web pages that look like text splashed on a computer screen. Today we see blinking icons, things that really do look like buttons, and strategic use of color. Visual cues help us pay attention to specific things, including things that advertisers want us to know or things that keep us safe.

Some visual cues have text and some do not. What they have in common is their graphic nature. Medina (2008) reminds us that vision trumps all of the other senses and is "probably the best single tool we have for learning anything" (p. 233). In other words, visual stimuli will be attended to over other stimuli most of the time, especially when the visual stimulus moves. Medina argues that attending to visual information is a survival mechanism, which is why it takes up so much neural real estate and resources (about 50 percent, according to Medina).

But all visual information isn't equal. Pictures consistently trump text or oral presentations. This tendency is so common that cognitive scientists have a name for it: pictorial superiority effect (Stenberg, 2006). For example, there is evidence that people can remember 2,500 pictures with about 90 percent accuracy several days after seeing them (Standing, Conezio, & Haber, 1970). In another study, adults were able to recognize pictures of Dick and Jane (from the readers) decades after they had completed elementary school (Read & Barnsley, 1977). It's not just that pictures are easier to remember; they're significantly more likely to be stored and much more likely to be retrieved.

Instructional visual cues tap into this effect. There's even evidence that visual cues are useful in teaching statistics (Burruss & Hecht, 2005). Visual cues to guide students' attention can be used in a number of ways, including cueing students to notice visuals, and creating graphic organizers.

Cueing Students to Notice Visuals

Sometimes the learner simply needs to be guided to the visuals that are already provided in a text. As Manning (2004) notes, teachers, especially of young children, "want students to utilize the pictures as well as the words to construct meaning about both fiction and nonfiction text" (p. 91). Manning also reminds us that examining the pictures or illustrations can activate students' background knowledge. But when students don't automatically do this, the teacher can provide a cue. For example, the teacher might use any of the following to cue the student to notice the visual information provided. You'll notice that some of these are phrased as questions, but that they aren't checking for understanding; instead, they are directing the students' attention to the visual information provided in the text:

- "Look at the cover of the book and predict what the story is about."
- "Based on the illustration, do you think the character is happy, sad, or scared?"
- "Looking through the book and noticing the photographs, what do you think is the author's purpose?"
- "The illustration on page 6 might be helpful in summarizing the text."
- "How might the story end? What is it in the illustrations that makes you think that?"
- "Take a look at this picture and think about the actions that take place."

Of course, directing students to the visuals isn't limited to the elementary school classroom. Mr. Burow has all of his 9th grade students create a website to store all of their course assignments, blog reflections, field notes, photo essays, and the like. In teaching students to create their own websites, he regularly projects a commercial website and cues his students about what to look for visually. For example, while projecting the *National Geographic* website, Mr. Burow cued students to notice some of the visual features of the page, including the use of color, the gigantic play button for the video feed, and the boxes and shading for different content areas. These cues help his students identify different aspects of construction that they might use in their own web pages.

Cueing Students to Action Based on Visuals

Sometimes we can cue students to do something with specific visuals. For example, when we write on a student's paper, we highlight errors that need to be corrected. When we circle a word, underline a sentence, or use a yellow highlighter, we're asking the student to pay attention to a specific aspect. These visual cues focus the student's attention on something that needs to be done. Of course, we do this in an electronic environment as well. We use the "track changes" function and virtual highlighting in word processing software to have the writer pay attention to a specific part of the paper.

In primary grade classrooms, visual cues are also used to teach students specific routines. For example, many kindergarten classrooms use a visual schedule that cues students what to do at specific times of the day so that they don't have to ask the teacher repeatedly. We also see tables labeled with specific colors that remind students about the task at that center. For example, the yellow table is for writing, and the green table is for sorting and counting activities. Further, some teachers in the primary grades use visuals to set boundaries in the classroom. The reading area might have yellow tape on the floor around it, whereas the desk area does not.

That's not to say that these types of visual cues aren't useful with older students. When we copy different sets of instructions for different projects on papers of certain colors, we're providing a cue that students can use later (e.g., "I know that I have to present orally, and those instructions were on light blue paper."). We've seen high school teachers use photographs of different tasks, paired with the text about the task, to ensure that all students, but especially English language learners, understand what is expected of them.

Texts also provide readers with visual cues that encourage them to take action. These are often referred to as text features as they cue the reader about things to notice and pay attention to. Bold words, for example, stand out on the page. Headings help us know that a new topic is being introduced. Figure 4.1 shows a list of text features, organized by the action they suggest.

Cueing Students with Graphic Organizers

Graphic organizers are tools designed to help students visually organize information to support their understanding. Graphic organizers are useful because they highlight important ideas and how they are related to one another. They are visual representations of a student's knowledge and are structured to show relationships through labels. Graphic organizers present information in concise ways to show key parts of the whole concept, theme, or topic and are highly effective for all students.

Graphic organizers help students pay attention to information and how it can be analyzed, synthesized, evaluated, and summarized. Alvermann and

Figure 4.1 | **Common Text Features That Cue Readers**

Elements That Cue Readers About the Organization of the Text
• Chapters
• Titles
• Headings
• Subheadings
• List of figures

Elements That Cue Readers to Locate Information
• Table of contents
• Index
• Page numbers

Elements That Cue Readers to Summarize and Synthesize
• Diagrams
• Charts and tables
• Graphs
• Glossary

Elements That Cue Readers to Visualize
• Photographs
• Illustrations

Elements That Cue Readers to Important Words
• Bolded words
• Italics and other changes in font

Boothby (1982) found that when students used a graphic organizer, they became more active readers; they paid more attention to the task at hand. When graphic organizers correspond with the text structure, they help students attend to the connections and relationships among concepts and ideas found in their reading.

There are four main types of graphic organizers, each with a specific use (Robinson, 1998): concept maps, flow diagrams, tree diagrams, and matrices.

Each type provides the student with a cue to be successful with the task at hand. See Figure 4.2 for a summary of how these organizers can be put into practice.

One of the great things about graphic organizers is that they serve as cues even when the teacher is not present. For example, Jaime completed a matrix about light, including various types of light (sunlight, candlelight, headlights, etc.) and characteristics of light (heat producing, incandescent, fluorescent, etc.). Her task was to analyze the types of light she encountered during the day. Jaime frequently referred to her matrix. This visual cue helped her complete the log and produce the work expected of her.

Graphic organizers can also be used in conjunction with teacher guidance to cue students. As part of their guided instruction, the students in Mr. Sleet's class construct graphic organizers as they read. For example, while studying the construction of the transcontinental railroad, students selected graphic organizers to help them take notes and visualize the information. Mr. Sleet teaches his students about the types of graphic organizers at the beginning of the school year and then invites them to choose the specific organizer that they think will help them consolidate the information. As he says, "If I'm always choosing the tools for my students, they'll never learn to do it. They need to determine which tool will work and how it aligns with the content and text structure. But I help them along the way, cueing and prompting them about what to choose and what to pay attention to."

When Micah selected a T-chart, a form of a matrix, to organize the information he was reading about Chinese immigrants' contributions to the railroad, Mr. Sleet asked him what the headings would be for the two columns in the chart. Micah answered, "Chinese and American." Mr. Sleet then asked Micah if the Chinese workers were Americans. Micah answered yes and realized that his categories weren't working out as he had expected. Micah scanned the text quickly to see if the text offered any organizational help. Understanding that the text provided a lot of details, Micah changed his choice from a T-chart to a concept map. When asked how he would label all of the circles, Micah said, "I'm starting with 'Chinese Americans Build a Railroad.' Then I can read and add ideas and branch them out. There are lots of details, so I think this will

Figure 4.2 | **Four Kinds of Graphic Organizers**

CONCEPT MAPS

Purpose: Describes the main ideas/concept, useful for brainstorming.

Description: Has the main concept in the middle of a page with lines from the central shape supporting the main concept with supporting details.

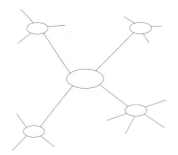

FLOW DIAGRAMS

Purpose: To show sequencing and time lines.

Description: Ideas are represented in shapes with arrows showing the direction or sequence.

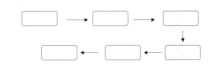

TREE DIAGRAMS

Purpose: Used to categorize and classify information; shows relationships and hierarchy.

Description: May be horizontal or vertical, with lines branching off the main concept into broad categories and lines branching off each category for more detailed information or supporting evidence.

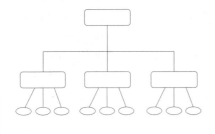

MATRICES

Purpose: To compare and contrast, shows relationships or classifies attributes.

Description: Words or phrases are arranged in a table format horizontally or vertically.

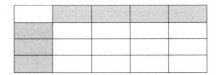

be better to help me remember." Satisfied that this tool would work, Mr. Sleet focused his attention on the next student as Micah got to work, reading and organizing his thinking.

Figure 4.3 shows a tool that can be useful in determining which graphic organizers to use and how to use them. Note that this planning tool extends beyond guided instruction, which is useful because guided instruction is only one part of a comprehensive instructional framework. Graphic organizers can also be used as part of whole-class modeling, in productive group work, or during independent learning tasks.

Verbal Cues

Verbal cues are the bread and butter of teaching, as we use our words to guide attention hundreds of times each day. Verbal cues often serve as hints or clues for students to use as they begin to integrate new learning into existing knowledge. They are also used to strengthen habits. We were intrigued by a study on the use of verbal cues to remind parents to buckle their young children into shopping carts (Barker, Bailey, & Lee, 2004). Most parents know to do this because it prevents falls, but until it becomes a habit, they may forget. The researchers posted a greeter at the store who said, "Have a nice day, and don't forget to buckle up" (p. 528). The use of the verbal cue resulted in increased use of the safety belt on the shopping cart.

Verbal cues are typically short and concise, as the intent is to shift attention to a key element. Often these cues are paired with other cues, such as when a teacher directs her students' attention to a language chart posted on an easel. A verbal cue may also be paired with verbal feedback, but they differ in intent. A verbal cue is designed to focus the student to accomplish something, whereas feedback is designed to increase the likelihood that the student does that thing again. Ormond (1992) calls this pairing of verbal cues and feedback a "package," such as when a verbal cue in a physical education class ("Contact the ball with the fingers") is combined with corrective feedback ("Don't palm the ball, just use your fingertips").

Figure 4.3	**Graphic Organizers Planning Guide**	
Topic of Study: _____	**Text Selection:** _____
Which type of graphic organizer will I use?	☐ Concept Map—Supports main idea or concept; helps with brainstorming ☐ Flow Diagram—Supports sequencing and time lines ☐ Tree Diagram—Helps categorize and classify information; creates a hierarchy ☐ Matrix—Helps to compare, contrast, or classify attributes
Introduce graphic organizer. How does it represent the structure of the text?	_____ _____ _____
When will the graphic organizer be used?	☐ Before reading ☐ During reading ☐ After reading
Guiding Questions—What questions will help the reader find important ideas?	☐ What is the key concept? ☐ What are categories that describe the key concept? ☐ How are they related? ☐ What is being compared? How are they similar or different? ☐ What are the critical events? How are they related? ☐ What are the stages or steps? How do they lead to each other? _____ _____ _____
How will students work on graphic organizers?	☐ Individually ☐ With partners ☐ Small group ☐ Whole group
How will students share graphic organizers?	☐ With partners ☐ Small group ☐ Whole group

Source: From *After School Content Literacy Project for California* (p. 104–105), by D. Fisher, N. Frey, and L. Young, 2007, Sacramento: California Department of Education. Reprinted with permission.

Verbal cues include those that highlight an error, such as when a teacher repeats what a student has incorrectly said so the student hears it. In addition, a verbal cue can use intonation to emphasize a point. When a teacher says, "Are you *sure* that's the next step to solve the problem?" he is employing intonation by stressing the word *sure*, with the intent of causing the student to pause. Figure 4.4 contains examples of verbal cues and techniques for emphasizing or highlighting errors.

As Arlyn Hackett circulates around his high school foods class, he provides numerous verbal cues for his students. They are preparing a chicken stir-fry and are now working at preparation stations. As he approaches a student who is cutting green peppers for the recipe, he says, "You can cut these into squares."

Figure 4.4 | Examples of Verbal and Emphasis Cues

Verbal Cues	Emphasis Cues
• "You need to underline…" • "Listen carefully to this next direction…" • "This is important…" • "Be sure to write this down in your notes…" • "Get your mouth ready to say this word." • "You said _____. Does that sound right?" • "Try that again." • "Try it another way." • "Look at that last part of that paragraph." • "The next step is…" • "This is a tricky part. Be sure…" • "Watch out! This is where lots of people make a mistake." • "Remember to…"	• Repeating a student's statement • Using intonation to stress a word or phrase • Slowing the rate of speech • Changing the volume of speech to emphasize a word or phrase • Pausing after beginning a statement to allow the student to complete the thought

He spots a student who is using a knife inefficiently to cut carrots and says, "When you put the knife point down, you can use the leverage and you won't work so hard." Janice is zesting an orange, and Mr. Hackett says, "You don't need to go that deep. Just go for the bright orange [of the peel]." Once the preparation of the ingredients is complete, several students are ready to operate the woks. Mr. Hackett has told them that speed is of the essence, and as their partners add ingredients, he cues them on the proper technique for handling the cooking spoons: "Stir! Stir! Toss! Toss! Up and over, down and under!" As the stir-fry ingredients sizzle, Mr. Hackett offers another verbal cue: "Now what you're looking for is for that chicken to be almost white." As the chicken cooks, he calls, "Peppers, peppers!" to cue them that it's time to add a vegetable. Before long, the class is sitting down to enjoy the fruits of their labor.

Gestural Cues

Gestural cues, those in which teachers motion with their body, are another way to alert the learner to important information or to draw attention to something that has been or might be missed. Gestural cues are a form of nonverbal communication. We all use nonverbal communication as we interact with one another; gestural cues simply formalize and perhaps exaggerate the information provided to students. Gestural cues work, in part, because they reduce the verbal overload that some students experience in the classroom. Remember that in most classrooms, teachers talk between 50 and 80 percent of the time (Flanders, 1970). Gestural cues cut through some of the talk and help students focus on specific components of the information.

Students can also be taught to use gestural cues to communicate with one another and their teacher. For example, reminding students to cross their fingers and not shout out when they have something they want to add to the conversation provides them with a personal gestural cue akin to tying a string around your finger to remember something. This gestural cue not only helps them remember, it also reduces impulsivity and alerts the teacher that specific students want to participate.

Gestural cues have a long history of effectiveness in teaching. For example, the Kodály Method of music teaching relies on Curwen hand movements as part of the instruction (Choksy, 1999). Curwen lived from 1816 to 1880 in England and recognized that gestural prompts would improve students' understanding of music. A sample page of Curwen hand movements appears in Figure 4.5. These gestural prompts are still used by music educators today. For example, we observed a choir instructor teaching students songs in Old English. They were not pronouncing the vowels correctly, and she placed her hand next to her mouth and sang the same vowel with her hand held horizontally and mouth open that way versus her hand held vertically and her mouth open that way. The sound is very different, and the students immediately made the connection.

But gestural prompts are not limited to music education. In a study of kindergarten students with and without disabilities who were learning new words, Weismer and Kesketh (1993) demonstrated the power of gestural prompts combined with speaking rate. Block, Parris, and Whiteley (2008) demonstrated that students learn comprehension processes via hand motions that portray these mental processes. These gestural cues, called Comprehension Process Motions (CPMs), focus on common comprehension strategies such as finding the main idea, making predictions, inferring, and clarifying. Block and her colleagues argue that CPMs work because they "make abstract, metacognitive aspects of comprehension processes visible, understandable, and accessible to young readers" (p. 469). Some people are even trying to teach robots to recognize human gestural cues (Bianchi-Berthouze & Kleinsmith, 2003).

Arzarello, Paola, Robutti, and Sabena (2009) argue that gestural cues are one of the resources students need to be successful in the mathematics classroom. They view gestures as "one of the semiotic tools used by students and teacher in mathematics teaching-learning" (p. 97). A sign or semiotic resource is anything that "stands to somebody for something in some respect or capacity" (Peirce, 1931/1958, vol. 2, paragraph 228), and can include speech, mathematical symbols, notes or other written language, and so on. An excerpt from the study by Arzarello and colleagues illustrates the role that gestural cues can play in teaching and learning. The students had worked in groups but had not

---

Figure 4.5 | Sample of Curwen Hand Movements

THE STANDARD COURSE.

MANUAL SIGNS OF TONE IN KEY.

NOTE.—*The diagrams show the hand as seen from the left of the teacher, not as seen from the front. Teachers should particularly notice this.*

soh

The GRAND or *bright* tone.

te

The PIERCING or *sensitive* tone.

me

The STEADY or *calm* tone.

doh

The STRONG or *firm* tone.

ray

The ROUSING or *hopeful* tone.

lah

The SAD or *weeping* tone.

fah

The DESOLATE or *awe-inspiring* tone.

For **fe**, let the teacher point his first finger horizontally to the left. For **ta**, ditto to the right. To the class these positions will be reversed, and will correspond with the Modulator. For **se**, let the teacher point his forefinger straight towards the class.

Source: John Curwen Standard Course (1904).

been successful with one of the problems: "Find the equation of the derivative of the function $fx = x^4 - 3x^3 + 4$" (2009, p. 104). A, L, and G are students, and T is the teacher:

T: So, you've written, f($x + h$) minus f(x) divided by h, what does it represent?

A: Practically it represents the slope at this point here [he is pointing at the point (x, f (x)) in the graph]. Because h is a wonderful invention that, practically, is a . . . it is a . . . it is an infinitesimal; not, not a true number, since it is something that is not zero, but at the end, we can exclude it, treating it almost as if it were zero, but it is not zero, otherwise, otherwise we would nullify (pointing at the numerator of the incremental ratio).

L: (Overlapping) It is so small (two pointed fingers, approaching each other), that it tends to zero (right hand moving horizontally, from left rightwards).

T: Eh! So, the smaller it is h (two pointed fingers) [. . .]

G: That is the more it is smaller, the more it is precise.

T: (Overlapping) The more we have information (thumb and forefinger touching) on the slope.

A: With numbers we could go always smaller, smaller, smaller. . . . We could choose the intervals always more, more . . . reduced, but we will never arrive to the precision level that is h. (Arzarello et al., 2009, p. 105)

The gestural cues focused students' attention on specific aspects of the problem, which in turn led to their successful completion of the task. As the authors of this study point out,

> gestures can play an important double role. First, as components of the semiotic bundle, they can support thinking processes of students.... Second, gestures have also a communicative function. This is true both concerning the teacher and the students. The teacher may use them as communicative tools in a conscious way. But gesture may play this role also for the students, even if in a less conscious way. In fact, they allow alternative ways of embodying and organizing information that the student is not able to express in purely verbal or formal ways. (Arzarello et al., 2009, p. 107)

Like CPMs, the gestural cues discussed here are multimodal, meaning that they involve more than one sense—which may help explain why they are effective. Gallese and Lakoff (2005) suggest that the sensory-motor system of the brain is multimodal rather than modular, as was previously thought. As they describe it,

> an action like grasping . . . (1) is neurally enacted using neural substrates used for both action and perception, and (2) the modalities of action and perception are integrated at the level of the sensory-motor system itself and not via higher association areas. (p. 459)

> Accordingly, language is inherently multimodal in this sense, that is, it uses many modalities linked together—sight, hearing, touch, motor actions, and so on. Language exploits the pre-existing multimodal character of the sensory-motor system. (p. 456)

In other words, although we cannot multitask, we can rapidly switch between modes and shift our attention accordingly. In doing so, we seem to pay more attention to stimuli that are referenced, especially with movement.

Physical Cues

Physical cues involve human touch, and this can make some people nervous. In fact, in some schools teachers are never allowed to touch a student. We assume we don't need to review good touch versus bad touch, but to be clear, we're talking about instruction using human touch. We're not talking about cultural situations in which specific students cannot be touched, as is the case with female Muslim students and male teachers. But touching is, in fact, one of the 15 interactions validated as effective for raising student achievement when "the teacher touches students in an appropriate, respectful, and friendly manner" (see Los Angeles County Office of Education, 2009).

There are a number of types of physical cues, from full physical guidance to a partial physical cueing, such as a light touch to encourage a response. What they all have in common is that they serve to divert the students' attention in some way. We're not talking about forcing students to complete a task based on our brute strength, but rather using touch to draw their attention to specific information. As Mally (2006) reminds us, cues of all types should be used to enhance student learning.

Let's consider a few examples of using physical cues to focus learners' attention. The first involves Ben, a student who has ADD/ADHD. As part of the guided instruction he receives, Nancy has to periodically place her hand on top of Ben's hand to refocus him on the task they're working on. This very simple physical cue signals Ben that there's something he should pay attention to. Similarly, kindergarten teacher Ms. Penrod places her hand over Kaila's hand and moves it to follow the specific words as they read together. This provides Kaila with the support necessary to pay attention to the correct word on the page as they read it. Here are some additional examples:

• Placing a hand on the student's shoulder to divert her attention to the left.

• Moving a student's hand down the pencil to hold it in the correct position.

• Offering a high-five or a handshake to focus the student's attention on a job well done.

Environmental Cues

As social animals, we're always sensitive to the environment, and we attempt to match our behavior to that environment. Each of us has internalized knowledge about the distance between people and the resulting appropriate communication style. Of course, this information is culturally influenced, but we all know a "close talker" when we meet one. In general, the distance between people engaged in communication cues them about the type of communication expected. Generally, in Western culture, it goes something like this:

• **Intimate distance**—Eighteen inches and closer. This distance allows you to lean in to make a private comment, give someone a hug, and speak in an informal and personal way. Slang is often used, and much of the communication is nonverbal.

- **Personal distance**—Eighteen inches to 4 feet. This distance is typically reserved for close friends, family, and some coworkers. This distance allows you to share information, but not information that is personal in nature. Typically, observers have a hard time following the conversation because much is already understood and is thus not explicitly stated.
- **Social distance**—Four to 12 feet. This distance shows respect for individual space when the relationship is not close. Personal information is not disclosed at this distance, and the communication patterns are more reserved, with talk typically focusing on socially appropriate topics.
- **Public distance**—Twelve feet and farther away. This distance is used for presentations of information, and the language register is expected to be more formal and academic.

Our point here is that the environment we're in sends us powerful cues about how to behave. If you doubt this, consider the evidence from nutrition studies. For example, Wansink and Sobal (2007) demonstrated the effect that an environmental cue (such as a large bowl) had on behavior. The study participants overate, but only 4 percent of them recognized that their overeating was due to the environmental cue. We're not here to talk about close talkers or overeating, but to harness the power of environmental cues.

Environmental Print

As teachers, most of us have walls within which we conduct our business, and we can use them for environmental cues that focus students' attention. There are a number of recommendations related to what teachers can use the wall space for, including word walls (Harmon, Wood, Hedrick, Vintinner, & Willeford, 2009), language charts (Roser, Hoffman, Labbo, & Farest, 1992), student work (Williams, 2009), and resources for completing tasks and assignments, including the purpose of the lesson (Fisher, Frey, & Rothenberg, 2008). Every single item on the wall should have one primary purpose, and that purpose should relate to student learning. In addition, items on the wall should be changed regularly. Our brains have an amazing ability to filter out a familiar stimulus (Elliott & Dolan, 1999). In fact, when an environmental cue becomes too familiar, we no longer even notice it!

Although we know that a print-rich environment is important, as Harmon and colleagues (2009) note, the "word wall itself does not teach" (p. 406), any more than a language chart or posted student work does; the teacher teaches. And part of that teaching involves using environmental cues to focus students' attention.

Mr. Crawford does this every time students in his class get stuck. He combines gestural and verbal cues with the environmental cues found in his classroom. Meeting with a group of students as they work, Mr. Crawford notices that they have not progressed and seem to be stalled on a process. They're supposed to be working collaboratively on writing and producing an iMovie based on a collection of poems they've assembled. Quickly assessing the situation, Mr. Crawford realizes that they haven't collected enough poems to complete the task. He asks, "How many poems do you have?" while he points to the large poster paper that has a checklist for the project. The checklist was developed with the students, so he knows that they're familiar with it, and it indicates that they must select at least 10 poems. Brandi says that they have only six poems. Jacqueline adds that they can't find "good ones" that fit their theme. Mr. Crawford looks over at the collection of poetry books sitting on a nearby table, walks over to get one, and says, "I know you can work this out. You've done a lot already, and you've shown me that when you put your mind to it, great things happen." They agree, and Michael adds, "We want ours to be the best, and we maybe gave ourselves too much pressure."

Leaving this group of students, Mr. Crawford joins the next group, which is working well. He looks at the students' work and then at the checklist. Smiling and giving a thumbs-up signal, he leaves the group to continue its work and joins the next group. They're not doing so well. They have more than 10 poems laid out in front of them. They also have a storyboard that is illustrated and contains text. But the students are not talking to one another; they're staring at laptop screens. Hypothesizing that they aren't sure how to use iMovie, Mr. Crawford walks over to a large poster labeled "Creating Your Movie." He points to the first step—"Connect a camera, open an iMovie project window, and import the video"—and says, "Is this already done?" Clearly the students are perplexed; they sit very still. He moves his hand down a bit to the illustration of the FireWire cable. As he does so, Antonio says, "Yeah, we got that. The FireWire is already connected. We've done it with every computer, but nothing seems to make it transfer." Mr. Crawford, pointing again to the first step on the poster, says, "Did you do all of this?" Sheepishly, Rocio says, "Not really. We didn't open the project window. I was thinking it did it automatically, like iTunes or iPhoto. Now I got it." She shows the rest of the group what she means, and they're off, working on their project once again.

Manipulatives and Objects

The materials we use in our classrooms are so ubiquitous that we rarely give them much thought. In primary classrooms, math and literacy manipulatives abound: an abacus, attribute blocks, Cuisenaire rods, Unifix cubes, magnetic letters, to name just a few. As students advance through the grades, teaching tools become more abstract and are more often represented by two-dimensional versions of three-dimensional ideas: notes, graphic organizers, textbooks, and such. However, manipulatives do not entirely disappear. Older students may use tangrams to understand geometric shapes or Styrofoam balls to simulate DNA structures, or create formulas using equipment in the chemistry classroom. Biology teachers routinely include dissections and lab experiments to help their students understand the structures and characteristics of organisms.

The use of manipulatives has a history in modern education that can be traced to the Montessori method. A central tenet of this approach, which dates back to the turn of the 20th century, is that learning occurs through the use of carefully designed objects that allow the learner to explore concepts. The legacy of this purposeful attention to objects can be found in nearly any current-day classroom. For example, algebra tiles are used to help students understand processes underlying calculations (Amdahl & Loats, 1995), object boxes with replications from ancient history are used to further students' understanding of important events (Gianetto & Rule, 2005), and toys are used to demonstrate physics principles (Guemez, Fiolhais, & Fiolhais, 2009). These hands-on activities serve to further scaffold instruction when they are used as an environmental cue.

Interactive whiteboards, which offer a means for manipulating two-dimensional representations of visual objects, can provide students with further cues for understanding concepts. For example, geometric concepts of area, space, and volume require that students move objects and stack them in space (Tan, 1994). This can be difficult to do in a large secondary class, and a teacher demonstration may be difficult for all students to view. However, an interactive whiteboard that allows students to move virtual objects in space can provide them with the experiences they need to fully grasp this concept (Hwang, Su, Hwang, & Dong, 2009).

Martha Ramirez uses manipulatives as cues each time she gathers her young students for guided math instruction. They are still gaining a sense of one-to-one correspondence and number sense, so the manipulatives she uses serve as an important cue for them. One student in the group, Eric, was having difficulty in properly adding 2 + 4 on his paper. Ms. Ramirez first used a visual cue, drawing circles representing the numbers on another piece of paper. She added a gestural cue, using the point of her pencil as she counted along with him. When the student still had difficulty, Ms. Ramirez moved from a visual cue to a manipulative one. She counted out four blue counting cubes and two yellow ones, then had Eric move them as both student and teacher counted together. She then asked Eric to do this alone, and he arrived at the correct answer. "I find it's a good progression to use," she said later. "There are times when they need to have that three-dimensional object in their hands."

Position

Sometimes the place where something is located in the environment also serves as a cue. Organizing the environment can cue learners to pay attention to specific things. But as Corsini (1972) has noted, position is likely confounded with verbal and nonverbal clues as well. By that we mean that position alone is often insufficient to attract the learner's attention. Having said that, position can be used as a trigger for memory. There's even evidence that our body position influences our memory. We recall information better if we hold our body in the same position as when we learned it. As Dijkstra, Kaschak, and Zwaan (2007) found, "Response times were shorter when body positions during prompted retrieval of autobiographical events were similar to the body positions in the original events than when body position was incongruent" (p. 139).

For example, an in-box near the door of the classroom signals students to submit their work there as they enter the room. A to-do list posted on the same spot on the board each day reminds students about the assignments that will be due this week. A signal to students to place their hands on the tops of their heads when the teacher needs their attention reminds each of them to stand quietly.

Sometimes moving something to a new position alerts the learner to pay attention and notice it anew. Nancy did this when she used position to cue a student so she could solve a tangram problem. She worked with Sophia, a 2nd grader who was having difficulty completing a chart for a mathematics lesson on geometric shapes. In preparation for future lessons involving tangram patterns, the teacher was instructing the students on finding simpler shapes. Sophia had the seven geometric shapes of the tangram spread before her, as well as a chart that required her to make specific figures using two or more tangram pieces. Sophia was stuck on finding two pieces that could form a parallelogram. She had successfully located a single parallelogram but then said, "There aren't two pieces." Nancy first used verbal cues, asking her to "look for the triangles," but Sophia was still stuck. Nancy then moved the two right triangles away from the pile and closer to the parallelogram. She offered another verbal cue: "Can you see the triangle shape inside the parallelogram?" When Sophia indicated that she could not, Nancy positioned the pencil in her hand so that it made a diagonal divide across the parallelogram. When Sophia still looked puzzled, Nancy positioned one of the right triangles on top of the parallelogram, leaving the other half of the single shape to be filled by the second triangle. After a pause, Sophia's eyes widened: "Oh! It's the two triangles!" Quite pleased with herself (and convinced she had done this alone), Sophia quickly drew two right triangles on the chart.

Summing Up

Research on the use of cues in learning shows that they have a positive effect on retention and transfer of information (deKoning, Tabbers, Rikers, & Paas, 2009). Teachers can use a number of cues to focus students' attention, including visual, verbal, gestural, physical, and environmental cues. Often cues are paired with prompts to ensure that students have the scaffolds they need to be successful. At other times, the cue is enough to ensure success.

As teachers, we use verbal cues regularly. But we must be conscious of the difference between cues and feedback. Although we can bundle verbal cues and feedback together, they serve different purposes for the learner. Cues focus learners' attention, whereas feedback provides learners with information about their success.

Gestural cues are important because they combine visual information with verbal information. Evidence indicates that gestural cues tap into the visual system, our primary way for gaining information. In addition to gestural cues, students notice environmental cues and physical cues, both of which are helpful in gaining attention.

Direct Explanation, Modeling, and Motivation

"Wait, you lost me."

That was Dan, a 10th grader in a three-dimensional art class, asking Mr. Hennessy, his teacher, to explain again a technique to successfully shape a wobbly lump of clay spinning on a potter's wheel. Although Dan had performed the first steps—throwing the clay on the wheel and using his wet hands to initially form it—he had not been able to center it. Until the clay was properly centered, Dan couldn't build a vase. Dan had watched Mr. Hennessy do this countless times as he demonstrated and modeled the process. Dan and the other students in the class were now engaged in their first experiences on the potter's wheel, and the teacher knew this was a critical juncture. As Dan's clay wobbled, Mr. Hennessy gave him several prompts ("Make sure you're using plenty of water so you don't create drag") and cues ("Put one hand on top and the other on the side of the clay and use your legs"), but Dan wasn't having any success. In fact, this last cue seemed to have the opposite effect—Dan stopped completely. Mr. Hennessy saw the look of puzzlement on Dan's face even before he said it.

"Wait, you lost me."

The teacher made a quick assessment of the situation and decided that he needed to provide some direct explanation and think aloud as he modeled. "Let's change places for just a minute," Mr. Hennessy told his student, who gratefully hopped down from the seat at the potter's wheel.

Mr. Hennessy: OK, talk to me, Dan. Let's figure out where the breakdown is. Can you tell me about the conditions you need and why?

Dan: Use lots of water so the clay spins. It should be smooth, like almost slippery. And make sure the wheel's got enough speed.

Mr. Hennessy: Why?

Dan: Um, centrifugal force. 'Cause it makes the clay center.

Mr. Hennessy: Well, partially right, but not completely. The spinning alone won't center it. You've also got to apply some pressure in a very specific way. [Mr. Hennessy turns the wheel back on, wets the clay, and gets ready.] Here's what I'm doing and why. I am going to brace my elbows against my thighs so my arms won't move. Then I'm going to cup my right hand on the side of the clay. I'm using that hand because it's my dominant hand. As I put a slight amount of inward pressure on the side of the clay, I'm going to bring my left hand onto the top of the clay. [As he speaks, he performs each of these actions.] Now I'm pressing *down* with the same amount of pressure as I am pressing *in*. But I'm being careful to use my legs. My arms would shake if I didn't have them steadied by my legs. So I've got three pressure points simultaneously: I'm pushing my elbows into my thighs, I'm pushing my right hand inward, and I've got my left hand pushing down. [As he speaks, the clay stops wobbling and begins to spin smoothly.] Now you try it with a new ball of clay. I know that this isn't easy, but once you get the hang of it, you'll love throwing clay.

Having benefited from his teacher's direct explanation, modeling, think-aloud, and motivation, Dan is ready to try again. He settles into the seat, turns on the wheel, throws the clay in the middle of it, and drizzles it with water. "Now remember what I said," the teacher says. He repeats the directions, this time prompting and cueing in time with Dan's actions. "Dig those elbows into your thighs," Mr. Hennessy reminds him. "Right, use your legs!" says Dan. "Now it makes sense!"

Defining Direct Explanation

Guided instruction, at its heart, is a dialogue between teacher and learner. However, at times the teacher must reassume cognitive responsibility and temporarily take it away from the learner in order to provide a direct explanation. Mr. Hennessy found that his prompts and cues were not enough for Dan at that moment in his learning. The teacher used questioning to check for understanding and rapidly hypothesized what Dan did and did not know. He then offered a direct explanation and modeled what he was doing as he thought aloud. He also acknowledged the difficulty of the task and encouraged Dan to be successful. Imagine—all of these complex teaching behaviors in the span of two minutes. But a well-timed direct explanation during guided instruction can result in improved student performance.

Direct explanation, modeling, and thinking aloud are closely related teaching behaviors that operate together. Alfassi (2004) says that "the teacher explicitly states which strategy is being taught and when it will be used. Then the teacher applies a think-aloud model that includes the reasoning involved in using the strategy, thereby revealing his or her ... processes" (p. 172). This is followed by guided practice that allows the student to assume increased cognitive responsibility and is accompanied by scaffolded instruction in the form of prompts and cues. The teacher monitors the application of the information by the student, checking for understanding through questioning, and using further direct explanation as needed (Duffy & Roehler, 1989).

It is useful to consider the kinds of knowledge that are needed to perform a task. Take virtually any skill and think about the ways you "know" about it. Let's use the nonacademic example of driving a car from Chapter 3. You possess declarative knowledge of the names, facts, labels, and lists associated with the skill. You can identify the steering wheel, parking brake, and rearview mirror, to name a few parts. In addition, you have procedural knowledge—the understanding of how to complete the task. Therefore, you know to adjust the mirror when you get in the car, place the key in the ignition, and release the parking brake. But there is a third type of knowledge we didn't discuss in Chapter 3—conditional—that is really what it takes to drive the car. In fact, your mastery of this complex skill comes with the acquisition of conditional knowledge. You understand when you need to use the parking brake on a steep incline, or why you dim your high beams when encountering another car. As learners acquire declarative, procedural, and conditional knowledge, they become more sophisticated in making decisions about what to do and how to do it, as well as when and why (Paris, Cross, & Lipson, 1984).

What does this have to do with direct explanation? In a word, *everything*. Effective use of direct explanation requires declarative, procedural, and conditional knowledge of the skill or concept (Duffy, 2003). In other words, the explanation should include the facts (declarative), the steps (procedural), and when or why to do it (the conditional). The three-part explanation provides the learner with a rationale for decision making, which is a hallmark of mastery and metacognition. It's important to recognize the kinds of knowledge needed for learning and for effective use of direct explanation. A study of five elementary core reading programs found that although items were often identified in the teacher's edition as "direct explanation," they commonly overlooked conditional knowledge (Dewitz, Jones, & Leahy, 2009). Published curriculum is of great value, but it cannot wholly substitute for deep teacher knowledge.

Direct explanation during guided instruction draws from the literature on direct instruction, including program design, organization of instruction, and student-teacher interactions (Watkins & Slocum, 2003). The difference is that direct instruction involves a specific script that the teacher reads. When used as part of guided instruction, in which the teacher is responding to the students' attempts to understand, scripting is nearly impossible. Remember, direct explanation is used when questioning to check for understanding has revealed a learning need and prompts and cues have not been successful in addressing that need. That's not to say that guided instruction is void of planning. The teacher has to have a purpose for the lesson and be on the lookout for misconceptions, misunderstandings, overgeneralizations, and oversimplifications. Many of these can be anticipated in advance, especially when the teacher has previous experience with students learning the content. That is where direct instruction can be useful.

Thompson (2009) defines direct instruction as "giving explanations, examples, or the answer; explaining the answer; referring to a previous discussion; posing a leading question for the student; and planning what the student should do next" (p. 427). Of course, this type of instruction can be used during other instructional phases, such as when first introducing information to students. But as part of guided instruction, when teachers are sharing responsibility with students, care has to be taken not to reassume control of the learning prematurely. Sometimes students wait for the teacher to tell them what to do because that's what they're used to doing. Seligman (1975) introduced a term that applies to this situation: "learned helplessness." In these situations, the student has learned to behave helplessly, believing that his or her behavior has no effect on the situation or outcome, even when the opportunity exists to change that situation or outcome. That's why we have to be judicious in moving to direct instruction or direct explanation in this phase of learning. We don't want to create or reinforce learned helplessness. Instead, we need to ensure productive success for students such that they learn the content and their actions can have an effect.

When the student does have an instructional need that cannot be addressed through prompts and cues, however, it is time to use direct explanations and modeling. In their review of direct instruction for comprehension, Coyne and his colleagues (2009) identified a number of factors important in this systematic approach, including conspicuous strategies, mediated scaffolding, strategic integration, primed background knowledge, and judicious review. We discuss each of these in the following sections.

Conspicuous Strategies

The conspicuous strategies component refers to the systematic teaching of important cognitive strategies "that makes them unambiguous and available to all students" (Coyne et al., p. 225). In part, this is done through teacher modeling for the whole class. For example, Ms. Jimenez modeled visualizing while reading aloud to the whole class from the science textbook. The class was focused on inherited traits, and at one point, Ms. Jimenez paused in the reading to say, "I'm seeing my grandmother's rose garden in my mind. I can visualize what the author is saying about different inherited traits. I see some of my grandmother's roses that grew tall and had beautiful petals. These lived a long time. I also see some roses that were not as tall as the other roses. The petals on those were not nearly as bright. They didn't live so long. As I visualize the whole garden, I see that rose plants close to the tree were the ones that weren't as tall or beautiful. I see what the author is trying to say about the environment having an impact on inherited traits."

But whole-class modeling is not the only time to provide students with conspicuous-strategy instruction. When they struggle, the teacher can provide a direct explanation of the strategy to specific students. This happened later in the lesson, when Ms. Jimenez was working with a small group of students at their table. Peter wasn't understanding the text, and Ms. Jimenez had attempted to scaffold his understanding through prompts and cues. She then asked Peter to look at the two flowers in the illustrations and consider what he knew about flowers to determine if they looked exactly alike. As she continued, she said, "Think about flowers you have seen, maybe in the park by school. They all seem to be the same, right? But they have little differences. Picturing those flowers in your mind, talk with your group about the differences, not the similarities."

Mediated Scaffolding

The second component identified by Coyne and his colleagues (2009), mediated scaffolding, focuses on the "initial, intentional, and temporary support provided to learners" (p. 228). Although they do not define the specific types of scaffolds, they remind us that these supports must be purposeful, in both their introduction and use. They also note that the supports must be withdrawn as students internalize and apply the knowledge. This mediated scaffolding requires the systematic use of questions, prompts, cues, and direct explanations to gradually shift responsibility from the teacher to the learner. It's also why teachers cannot simply tell students what they want them to know; learning just doesn't work that way.

Strategic Integration

As students become increasingly skilled in specific cognitive strategies, the teacher has to ensure that they learn to "integrate and relate new information, concepts and strategies" (Coyne et al., 2009, p. 231), as learning requires more than rote memorization of facts or procedures. This strategic integration allows students to solve problems and think critically. Although teachers might focus on one cognitive strategy at a time during an introduction, integration of these strategies is important for subsequent independent use. In other words, focusing for four weeks on the reasonableness of an answer in mathematics will not ensure that students understand how this procedure fits into their overall problem-solving scheme. Similarly, focusing for four weeks on predicting what will happen next in a book will not ensure that students also infer, make connections, question, and summarize as they read complex pieces of text. This is what guided instruction is all about: helping students integrate what they have learned with the support necessary to be successful.

Again, this is why guided instruction is hard to script in advance. When Andrew got stuck on his essay and prompts and cues were not helping, he needed to be reminded to return to the question he was trying to answer and compare that with the book he was reading. As Mr. Gutierrez said to him, "You're stuck on summarizing, but that's not the only thing you know how to do. Remember that you can visualize and let your reader in on what you see. You can also make connections with your own experiences and those presented by the author. Reread the question again and think about what you know and what you've read as you consider your response. I know this isn't easy, because there are lots of ways to answer the question. It's your answer that matters. And your answer must be a balance between the book you've read and your own thinking."

Primed Background Knowledge

As we have noted previously, students differ in a number of ways, including in what they already know and have experienced (Fisher & Frey, 2009a). Coyne and his colleagues (2009) note that "priming, or activating, background knowledge helps students relate new information and strategies to their prior knowledge and experiences" (p. 235). Teachers develop and activate background knowledge throughout the lesson, not just during guided instruction. For example, while reading to the whole class from the science text about inherited traits, Ms. Jimenez modeled her use of activating background knowledge by saying, "I was thinking about what I already know. I know that I inherited traits from my parents just like new plants inherit traits from their parents. I'm wondering why my sisters and I don't look exactly alike since we have the same parents. I inherited hazel eyes, but my sisters both have brown eyes." Sometimes, background knowledge interferes with understanding. Students sometimes draw on their experiences and get confused with the new content. You'll see this in the conversation Ms. Jimenez had with a group of students when they got stuck on the concept of "population" in their science book; they had different understandings of the word based on what they brought to the table, and this information was interfering with their understanding.

Ms. Jimenez: I hear that you're all stuck. Did you look at the word wall for help?

Jesus: Yeah. But I don't get it. What does it mean, *group*?

Ms. Jimenez: A collection of the same thing.

Maria: Like our books in the library?

Ms. Jimenez: Yes, books can be part of a group. And we do call the library a collection. But the word we're really focused on is *population*. And population is a group, but a group of the same kind of living thing.

Jesus: Like things in the environment?

Chris: Air.

Paul: Trees.

Chris: Sunlight.

Paul: Birds.

Maria: Water.

Jesus: Food.

Paul: Flowers.

Ms. Jimenez: Oh, I'm hearing some confusion here. Remember that I said that the word *population* is used for *living* things. I'm going to think about a number of groups of things; and then I'll think about which ones can be a population, because they're living, and which cannot. Here's my list: *tables, air, students, roses, pencils, clothes, hamsters,* and *dogs.* I'm going to make a T-chart so that I can have two columns—one for living things and one for nonliving things. *Tables* are not alive, so that goes in the "nonliving" column, and I can't use population. *Air* is something we need to live, but it's not alive so it also goes into the "nonliving" column, and I know that I can't say that there is a population of air. *Students* is next, and you're all living. I can say that I have a population of students. It goes in the "living" column. [The conversation continues through the list.] Now you try it. Here are a few more for you to classify. Use your whiteboards. This takes some thinking, but we have time to get this right. Try these: *teachers, sunlight, dolphins, computers, photographs, volcanic rocks,* and *geese.* [The students get to work, and Ms. Jimenez monitors their success, ready to provide scaffolds as necessary.]

Judicious Review

The final component necessary for student success, according to Coyne and his colleagues (2009), involves providing students with repeated opportunities to practice, develop, and apply their knowledge and skills. They note, "Review is most effective when it is sufficient, distributed, cumulative, and varied. Review is sufficient when a student can perform a task automatically and fluently" (p. 238). When the student can perform the task or skill automatically and fluently, the teacher has to remember to fade the scaffolds. This is an important aspect, and one that can be easily overlooked.

Judicious review requires that teachers notice what students know and can do and then use that information to plan lessons. Judicious review also requires that teachers sequence learning so there are opportunities for spiral review, because long-term retention is better when learning and review are distributed rather than concentrated. As with the other components identified by Coyne and his colleagues, judicious review is not limited to guided instruction. The sequence of learning and teaching extends through modeling, productive group work, and independent tasks. But guided instruction can be used to reinforce the skills and strategies that are being developed. Again, this is why it's hard to script a guided instruction lesson. When the student successfully responds, either to a question to check for understanding or to the use of a prompt or cue, the teacher does not move to direct explanation. But when this does not work to ensure productive success and the student is at risk of learned helplessness, the teacher moves into direct explanation based on need, including skills, strategies, procedures, or tasks that the student has already learned.

Defining Modeling

One of the most powerful tools in a teacher's repertoire is modeling. We define modeling as a demonstration of a skill or problem-solving strategy by an expert (Fisher, Frey, & Lapp, 2009). Students are able to witness how the expert (teacher) applies his or her deep knowledge to complete the task. Modeling is regularly used in the visual and performing arts and in athletics because demonstration is so vital. It is also used in other disciplines that draw on less visible skills, such as reading, writing, and mathematics. In reading comprehension, a teacher might model how a passage is understood, or how text features such as a diagram or a subheading support that understanding. A teacher modeling writing might demonstrate how an indentation signals a new paragraph, or the way a writer uses adjectives to bring a scene to life. In mathematics, the teacher might model the steps in an algorithm, separating relevant from irrelevant information in a word problem, estimating an answer based on the information given in a problem, or determining the reasonableness of the answer after solving a problem.

The efficacy of modeling may have a neurological basis as well. In the 1990s, Giacomo Rizzolatti and other neuroscientists began to explore the functions of specialized neurons that played a part in hand and mouth operations. They dubbed these *mirror neurons* because they found that these cells were activated in the brains of macaque monkeys who watched another monkey perform tasks such as grasping a piece of fruit. A series of experiments led to an understanding that these mirror neurons work together in systems that activate pathways throughout the brain and assist with recognition of various actions. Other researchers have subsequently explored these mirror neurons in humans. You'll recall from Chapter 4 our discussion of another series of studies that was done with ballet and capoeira dancers, who were able to notice the technical movements of fellow dancers in their field with greater accuracy. These same studies also looked at brain activation patterns and found that the pathways were similarly triggered in the people doing the dancing and those who were witnessing it (Calvo-Merino et al., 2005).

So what does the mirror neuron system have to do with teacher modeling? Although the links are still speculative, there is the possibility that the act of witnessing a behavior may assist with establishing initial pathways in the brain. These pathways must be strengthened through repeated use, and witnessing alone will not fully teach a skill. However, it is intriguing to consider the way preliminary demonstrations can over time build pathways that become more fluent with practice. Some neuroscientists writing for the popular press are themselves speculating about the possible role of mirror neuron systems in understanding the intentions of others (Iacoboni, 2008).

Of course, we are not suggesting that the neurosciences should drive educational practice, but rather that knowledge of current research about the brain can strengthen and deepen our knowledge of why effective instructional practices work. We are not suggesting that merely demonstrating something will lead to student learning. In fact, in the absence of the expert pointing out what to notice, it is likely that the student will notice the wrong things, or even come away from the demonstration with a misconception of what took place (Roth, McRobbie, Lucas, & Boutonne, 1997). They need what Coyne and his colleagues (2009) call the mediated scaffolding that occurs when the teacher models and draws the learner's attention to the decision making that occurred before, during, and after the skill or action occurred. Students need to witness the teacher's thinking firsthand and see the interaction of both the cognitive and the metacognitive aspects required to successfully apply the skill or action.

A modeling scaffold is further enriched through the use of a think-aloud process. Eley and Norton (2004) looked at a series of instructional arrangements for teaching mathematical procedures and found that demonstrations accompanied by if-then explanations that describe the relationship between the rule and the conditions for using it, or the rule and its relationship to the goal or intention, were more effective. When Mr. Hennessy explains to his student in his pottery class, "Here's what I'm doing and why," he is linking the rule with the condition. When Ms. Greenfield says to her kindergarten students, "I know it helps my readers if I make a picture to go with my story; I'm going to draw a picture of the cat and the bird in my story," she is linking the goal to the rule. These teacher think-alouds provide a further extension of what can be done during guided instruction when prompts and cues have not resulted in student understanding.

Teacher Think-Alouds

A think-aloud is a verbal protocol for explaining one's decisions while performing a task (Davey, 1987). This verbalization of the inner monologue that occurs in the teacher's mind can significantly help students who mistakenly attribute the teacher's knowledge to "being smart." In other words, students often think that their teachers "just know stuff" and that we adults do not work to understand the things we're doing. Students who are at risk for failure disproportionately believe that what a person knows is a fixed variable and outside one's control. As teachers, we understand that knowledge is not innate, but rather is something that is actively built. Teacher think-alouds can help to disrupt this misconception that one either knows something or doesn't. By thinking aloud, we expose the cognitive moves, including the fits and starts, that one goes through in arriving at conclusions.

A teacher think-aloud is also specific in directing students where and when a specific problem-solving strategy or procedural step should occur. Block (2004) demonstrated the strong desire students have to understand their teachers' thinking. She surveyed more than 600 6th grade students who identified the things they most wanted to know from their teacher in regard to written text. The things mentioned most frequently were the following:

- Describing what the teachers did to understand an occurrence in the text
- Demonstrating how the teachers knew when they had the correct meaning for the word
- Demonstrating how the teachers applied specific reading processes

Although these responses are specifically about reading, they are instructive in determining the elements of an effective teacher think-aloud during guided instruction. To start, the teacher alerts students to the methods used to form an initial global understanding of a problem, situation, or task. For instance, Ms. Hunt tells her 6th grade social studies students:

> **Ms. Hunt:** When I first thought about the pharaohs of Egypt and the enslavement of the Israelites, I wondered about how they could manage to treat people in such a way. I was thinking to myself, "Didn't the pharaohs see the suffering around them?" I know that when I learn about an event in history that seems unimaginable to me, I have to take a step back and ask myself some questions about why it would seem reasonable to a person of the time. And then I began to realize that maybe the pharaohs saw it but weren't moved by it because they believed that the enslaved people weren't really people but rather were there to serve.

Obviously Ms. Hunt is focusing students on how she gains an initial understanding of a situation. Another discipline might involve witnessing the chemistry teacher's way of locating information in the periodic table, or listening to a 1st grade teacher explain how she makes some initial choices about selecting a book according to its title and cover. In all cases, the think-aloud is focused on a global understanding, not on the details.

A second type of think-aloud concerns how one knows whether a decision is correct or not. For instance, while 10th grade English teacher Mr. Fontaine is composing a summary paragraph, he says the following:

> **Mr. Fontaine:** I knew I wanted to get these facts into my summary: that Sandra Cisneros is the author of the book *The House on Mango Street*, that she wrote it in 1984, and that she writes in a unique style that might seem simple but really isn't. But I know that if I just say that—you know, that it's a simple style and I don't explain it—then it's not much of a summary. If I were reading this, I would want to know more. Because you don't just get to say that and not give a justification or a rationale or an example or *something*. When I write, I have to keep the reader in mind. That's how I check my own writing. What would I want to know if I were reading this for the first time?

Mr. Fontaine is alerting his students to how he makes judgments about the correctness of his actions. A physical education teacher might think aloud about the way he looks for the topspin of the tennis ball he strikes as a determinant for whether his serve was optimal or not. An elementary mathematics teacher might think aloud about how she checks her answer to an equation to see if she gets the same number twice.

A third method for thinking aloud involves showing students how you use a particular process or procedure to accomplish a task. In the following example, Ms. Lyons thinks aloud as she assembles materials to assist a 5th grade student in completing a circuit to light a lightbulb:

Ms. Lyons: Of course, the best way to know if I did this correctly [completed a circuit] is to see the lightbulb light up. But as I'm building the circuit I have to keep checking in to see if I've got everything in place. I need to make sure I have all the materials first or it isn't going to work. I have to make sure that the wire has full contact with the battery. I know that if it doesn't, it won't work. So I'm going to use this black electrical tape to hold it in place so it doesn't slide off. And I know that to make it a full circuit, I have to make it go all the way around [gestures in a circular fashion]. So I need one wire that goes from the negative terminal to the bulb. And I've got another wire that goes from the bulb to the positive terminal. That's what I do before I get started. I make sure I have everything I need.

In this example, Ms. Lyons modeled using the strategy of assembling the correct materials to a student who had not done so. Her previous prompts ("What are you missing?") and cues ("Take a look at what Roberto has on his desk") didn't work, so she used a think-aloud to model how she thinks through the process to determine the materials she needs. A middle school reading teacher might model asking himself questions to monitor his understanding when reading a poem. A high school history teacher might think aloud as he refines a search of documents on the Japanese internment camps of World War II that are stored in the online database of the National Archives. In each case, the teacher think-aloud focuses on an important detail that is intended to help a student move to the next step.

Thinking aloud in mathematics is similar to thinking aloud in other disciplines, although that fact may not seem apparent at first. The emphasis in supporting mathematical thinking is on correct calculation, to be sure, but there is more to it than that. Other vital aspects of mathematics include estimating an answer in advance of the calculation and deciding whether the answer makes sense. Examples of thinking aloud in mathematics include the following:

- Background knowledge (e.g., "When I see a triangle, I remember that the angles have to add to 180°.")
- Relevant versus irrelevant information (e.g., "I've read this problem twice and I know that there is information included that I don't need.")
- Selecting a function (e.g., "The problem says 'increased by' so I know that I'll have to add.")
- Setting up the problem (e.g., "The first thing that I will do is … because …")
- Estimating answers (e.g., "I predict that the product will be about 150 because I see that there are 10 times the number.")
- Determining reasonableness of an answer (e.g., "I'm not done yet as I have to check to see if my answer makes sense.") (Fisher, Frey, & Anderson, 2010, pp. 150–151)

Regardless of the discipline, the purpose of a teacher think-aloud during guided instruction is to provide a well-timed scaffold to move the student to the next step or stage. In addition, the teacher think-aloud is an initial step, not an end point. In keeping with a gradual release of responsibility, the student think-aloud is the other part of this dialogue. It can provide you with evidence that students understood what was modeled, or that they require more assistance.

Student Think-Alouds

The think-aloud protocol originated as a methodological tool for gaining insight into the mind of a research subject. It is widely used in diverse fields such as marketing, product design, and computer science. Psychologists have adopted think-alouds as a way of understanding how a complex academic task is understood. For example, the well-known "writing process" literature (brainstorm, draft, edit, draft, revise, publish) stems from work by Janet Emig (1971), who used a think-aloud process with 12th grade writers to gain insight into the way they composed. Student think-alouds can provide teachers with evidence of the extent to which students are learning what has just been explained, modeled, demonstrated, or taught through a teacher think-aloud. It is the next instructional move in a sequence. Wilhelm (2001) suggests that an extension of the teacher think-aloud comes in the form of a student first monitoring and helping out. This participation comes at the invitation of the teacher, as the student may otherwise think he is interrupting. For instance, as the teacher thinks aloud about solving a word in a text using context clues, the student responds by saying, "Got it. So you looked at the paragraph before this one to find the sentence where that word was in bold letters." This exchange lets the teacher know that the student was monitoring both the content of the teacher think-aloud and the intent of it.

The teacher can also invite the student to assume more of the cognitive load by asking him to notice how he resolves a problem. When the student, at the behest of the teacher, says, "The first thing I did on this word problem was to ask myself what the problem was asking me to solve," he is displaying an understanding of the content and his metacognitive awareness of how he approaches a word problem in mathematics. In other cases, the student's inability to explain, or his incorrect explanation, can provide evidence of what needs to be taught next. If the student says, "The first thing I did when I saw this word problem was write down the numbers so I could solve it," the teacher is alerted to the likelihood that the student's logic is faulty and will probably lead him to an incorrect answer because he is ignoring the details. In either case, the student think-aloud in guided instruction serves as a means for determining whether to move on or return to further direct explanation and modeling.

Defining Motivation and Encouragement

The role of motivation in learning has been of ongoing interest to educators for decades. Motivation is thought to be closely linked to one's ability to set goals, use problem-solving strategies, persist in the face of difficulty, and intrinsically reward oneself for achieving a goal. In addition, the relative amount of motivation a student has for a particular task can mean the difference between being resilient when a failure occurs or simply giving up (Zimmerman, 2008).

Motivation is a multifactor construct that is influenced by a number of things, such as general interest in the subject matter, perception of the usefulness of the information, general desire to achieve, self-confidence and self-esteem, patience, persistence, and choice (Davis, 1993). But not all students are equally motivated, or motivated by the same things. Brophy (1987) reminds us that motivation to learn is a competence acquired "through general experience but stimulated most directly through modeling, communication of expectations, and direct instruction or socialization by significant others (especially parents and teachers)" (n.p.). We could, of course, engage in a conversation about the differences between, and relative merits of, intrinsic and extrinsic motivation, but that's beyond the scope of this book (for more information, see Brophy, 2010). For our purpose here, we need to consider the ways in which student motivation can be addressed as a scaffold. Teachers can ensure that their guided instruction includes motivation scaffolds, which Thompson (2009) defines as "acknowledging that the task is difficult; using humor; providing positive and negative feedback; reinforcing correct responses from students by repeating them; helping students maintain motivation and control frustration through sympathy and empathy" (p. 428).

We've included the discussion of motivation scaffolds here, even though they can be used in every part of guided instruction, because of their relative importance when the teacher has reassumed control of the learning. That's not to say that we don't think motivation scaffolds aren't important as part of prompting or cueing, but rather that they are critical when students are experiencing difficulty and the teacher has moved into direct explanation and modeling.

Motivation scaffolds really can be as simple as acknowledging that the task is difficult. Here are some illustrative quotes from teachers at various grade levels:

- "When I first learned this, it took me hours to get it."
- "This is hard work we're doing. Most people don't know how to solve these kinds of problems."
- "I understand how hard this is, and I appreciate your focus on learning."
- "Just looking at this problem gives me jitters, but I know we can solve it."
- "The words this author uses are hard. I have to use a dictionary when I'm reading his work. But it's so worth it; the prose he uses is just delicious."

In addition to acknowledging the difficulty of the task, motivation scaffolds involve feedback. The research on feedback indicates that it is a powerful way to improve student learning, especially when it is directly related to specific goals or objectives that the students understand (Hattie & Timperley, 2007). The best feedback provides students with information about their progress or success and what course of action they can take to improve their understanding to meet the expected standard (Brookhart, 2008). And feedback is motivating because students want to know how they're doing; they easily see through false praise. Here are some examples of feedback that serves to motivate students:

- "Wow! That twist in your story really caught my attention. I hope you'll do that again."
- "I'm confused right here. Who is this we're talking about? I think you'll want to clarify which person is talking."
- "Are you proud of yourself? Not only did you make a convincing argument, you stood proud while you spoke."
- "I found several mistakes in this. It's not like you to make these types of mistakes. Would you like to try it again?"

In addition, motivation scaffolds can involve repeating correct responses so that students will repeat them. Maloch (2002) calls these "reconstructive caps," in which the teacher recounts what has happened, and "by doing so, she [the teacher] made their discussion process more visible to her students and thus, most likely, made it more understandable. There was also an evaluatory tone in which she positively reinforced this process, encouraging students to engage in these practices in future discussions" (p. 105). Here are some examples of this type of motivational scaffold:

- "Right. Using your function key is a shortcut that helps us focus on the task at hand."
- "When Tristen said that, I noticed that he made eye contact with various people in the room. He also made his point clearly so that we could all evaluate it and determine if we agreed or disagreed."
- "You used the sentence frame when you reported on your findings, which really helped you focus on the academic words."

The final type of motivation scaffold involves empathy and sympathy, the type of interactions we should have with students. This scaffold requires that we demonstrate our understanding that students' responses are based on what they currently understand. These interactions, if they are to serve as motivation scaffolds, have to be built on a very trusting relationship between the teacher and the students. Most important, sarcasm is avoided. Simply said, most students don't understand sarcasm and are hurt by the comments (Lewis, 2001). The *American Heritage Dictionary* defines *sarcasm* as "a cutting, often ironic remark intended to wound" and "a form of wit that is marked by the use of sarcastic language and is intended to make its victim the butt of contempt or ridicule." From its Latin and Greek roots it means "to bite the lips in rage." Although sarcasm might be OK between friends, it violates the motivation scaffold because it's intended to hurt. Just think about comments made to students such as "I'm shocked to get this paper; yours are never on time" or "Look who's graced us with her presence" and what they are intended to communicate—humor for the class at the expense of one student. That's not to say that teachers should avoid humor. Humor is a great motivational scaffold. Humor—not at the expense of another person—builds the relationship between students and teachers; sarcasm destroys it. Examples of humor, empathy, and sympathy include the following:

- "That makes my head hurt when I have to think that hard! How about you?"

- "I know that your dad is still sick. What can I do to help you?"
- "You're working really hard, and your work is paying off."
- "I feel your pain. I'll be here after school if you want to talk or get some help."

Summing Up

The need to reassume the cognitive load during guided instruction should never be viewed as a failure, but rather as a wholly expected instructional move that is likely to be required in any teaching event. In some cases, prompts and cues resolve the error or misconception and direct explanations are not necessary. When questions, prompts, and cues don't lead to desired results, the scaffolds associated with direct explanation, modeling, and motivation can provide students with both the intellectual material they need to move to the next step and the encouragement to persist when the task is hard.

6

Answers to Questions on Considerations and Logistics

This book has focused on guided instruction that provides students with the instructional scaffolds they need to be successful. Guided instruction requires that teachers consider what the student knows and what the student still needs to know. It's part of a comprehensive framework for instruction that includes establishing purpose and modeling, productive group work, and independent learning tasks. That's not to say that guided instruction is easy to implement. Teachers need routines for using questions to check for understanding, and for applying prompts and cues to scaffold student learning. When students still struggle, teachers need to know how to use direct explanations, modeling, and motivation to kick-start the learning. To implement guided instruction, teachers have to know how to group students. This chapter focuses on the questions we're often asked as teachers validate and extend their guided instruction efforts.

Can Guided Instruction Be Used in Whole-Class Instruction?

Of course guided instruction can be done with the whole class, and we have provided examples of this throughout this book. Again, it's the intent that we're interested in. When teachers question to check for understanding, prompt, cue, explain, model, and motivate, they're engaged in guided instruction. What we have to be careful about in using guided instruction with the whole class is that some students check out when the teacher focuses on one student. With whole-class guided instruction, the questions have to be posed in such a way that each student is accountable for responding. This can be accomplished with personal dry-erase boards, partner conversations, audience-response systems, thumbs up/down, and a host of other instructional routines. That's not to say that one student won't be called on to respond, but rather that all students are engaged in the questioning to check for understanding. Based on the responses to the question, the teacher uses prompts, cues, direct explanations and modeling, and motivation to share the cognitive work with students. Again, inclusive participation is critical. When guided instruction turns into an individual helping situation between the teacher and one or two students, instructional time is lost for the rest of the class. In those situations, students would be better off engaged in productive group work and independent learning tasks, which free up time for the teacher to guide students who need it. Although guided instruction can, and should, be used for whole-class instruction, getting to smaller needs-based groups is critical if we expect to get breakthrough results. The evidence is clear: students need guided instruction from their teachers that is based on what they already know and still need to learn. And that's where grouping enters the picture.

How Should Students Be Grouped for Guided Instruction?

The quick answer to this question is *intentionally*. There should be a reason that each student is in the group. The longer answer depends on what the other students in the class are doing while guided instruction is occurring. Let's address the grouping that occurs in a productive group work task first, since this is often key to grouping for guided instruction. The groups should be diverse because when students are away from the teacher, they rely on one another to be successful. As part of their interaction, productive group members share information and experiences, thus building each other's background knowledge. Ability grouping for productive group work does not result in increased achievement and can be harmful in terms of students' self-esteem and self-efficacy (Flood, Lapp, Flood, & Nagel, 1992; Oakes, 2005).

We use alternate ranking most often in our own classrooms when creating productive groups that are working away from the teacher. This approach ensures that each group is diverse in terms of knowledge and skill. Of course, if two students have had a conflict, recently broken up, or something of that nature, we wouldn't put them in the same group. We compose a list of students in rank order of their academic scores and social skills, yielding a cumulative overall score. For example, a student may rank as number 1 in academic skills, but number 21 in social skills, for an overall score of 22. Using the overall scores, we rank-order them from highest to lowest and divide the list in two equal portions. For instance, students 1 through 15 are on the first list, and students 16 through 30 are on the second. We then compose productive work groups by partnering student number 1 with student 16, student 2 with student 17, and so on. This gives us partners that are heterogeneous, yet not so far apart that they have difficulty bridging the divide. We can also form groups of four by having two consecutive students from each list (such as students 3 and 4 and students 18 and 19) form a group. Although not completely foolproof, this method does give us a starting point for creating productive work groups systematically.

As an example, Mr. Bautista created a list of his 30 students in order of their performance on a recent formative assessment. Brandi received the highest score, followed by Destini. In the middle at number 16 was Raquel. Number 17 was Tyler. Given that Mr. Bautista has more female students in his class than males, this group worked. Student number 18, Araceli, had recently broken up with student number 3 on the list, so it didn't make sense to put them in a group together at this point. Mr. Bautista decided to trade positions 18 and 20, adding Araceli to a different group.

Here's where guided instruction comes in. As the teacher who is engaged in guided instruction, you can insert yourself into the productive work groups and question, prompt, cue, explain, or model. In doing so, you assess student understanding and scaffold learning. In your absence, while you're working with other groups, the students rely on one another and their understanding of the task to complete the assignment. As an example, Mr. Thomas's students were working in reciprocal teaching groups reading a primary source document ("Give Me Liberty or Give Me Death," Patrick Henry, March 23, 1775). The students understood their task and were engaged in conversations using questioning, clarifying, summarizing, and predicting (Palincsar & Brown, 1984). Mr. Thomas moved from group to group, guiding students' thinking. He stopped at one group as they were discussing the paragraph that starts with "Mr. President, it is natural to man to indulge in the illusions of hope." Mr. Thomas enters the conversation with a question to check for understanding ("Why would Mr. Henry say that it's natural for humans to have hope?"). The four students in the group have answers for this, mostly from their background knowledge and experiences. For example, Katrina responds, "If people didn't have hope, they wouldn't accomplish much. Hope keeps us motivated."

Satisfied that they understand part of the quote, Mr. Thomas asks another question, "Let's talk about two of the words specifically in this quote: *indulge* and *illusions*. Why does he use those terms? How does that connect with the rest of the paragraph?" The students look confused, and Mike offers, "I think he says *illusion* because there really isn't hope for what he wants." Sebastian says, "Illusion is fake, not real. It's a negative to have illusions. I think he's really saying that hope is fake." Mr. Thomas prompts students to consider the context of the quote: "Think about the time this was written. It's 1775. It's not yet 1776."

Jessica says, "Yeah, that's it. They're trying to gain independence. He's saying that it's natural to hope; humans gotta hope. It's not a negative; it's human nature." Sebastian adds, "Oh, wait. That's what it means. He says some people 'shut our eyes against a painful truth,' meaning that we create an illusion that isn't really there. He wants to get all of the information." Mr. Thomas cues the students by pointing to the last line of the paragraph, pausing his finger at the word *anguish*. Katrina adds, "So he knows that the information will cause stress, but he wants to know it all so that he can be prepared." Satisfied that they're back on track, Mr. Thomas leaves them to their work and moves to the next group.

Alternatively, the teacher can identify specific students to meet with for guided instruction. While the rest of the class is engaged in productive group work or independent tasks, the teacher calls specific students to her desk for additional guided instruction. The students who meet with the teacher are identified based on instructional needs, not a perception of their ability. When the teacher is there to guide instruction—and we mean physically present with the learners in the group—it makes sense to have students with common learning needs working together.

For example, as part of their math instruction, students in Ms. Brandywine's class work in productive groups of four to create collaborative posters on which they solve the problems with words, numbers, and illustrations. Students use different-colored markers to ensure individual accountability. Ms. Brandywine identifies specific students based on their instructional need to join her at the teacher table. One of the groups still needs review on number sense. These four students meet with their teacher for guided instruction while the rest of the class continues working on their posters. This guided instruction group is needs-based in that every student in the group has a similar instructional need. When they finish the guided instruction with their teacher, the students return to their productive groups to work on their collaborative tasks.

In both examples—guided instruction that occurs within a productive work group, or guided instruction that occurs with a specially formed small group of learners—the constant is the role the teacher plays in providing instructional scaffolds. We don't subscribe to the belief that differentiation begins and ends with forming groups. It is the active role teachers take as they interact with the group that is a vital element in being able to differentiate instruction through questions, prompts, cues, direct explanation, modeling, and motivation.

How Should Groups Be Formed?

Groups can be formed a number of ways, depending on the task. As we plan instruction, we think about the three most common ways that teachers can form groups:

- **Teacher choice**, in which the teacher assigns specific students to groups, is the most common grouping format for productive group work and guided instruction.
- **Student choice** is another way to group. This arrangement works well for tasks that are completed outside of school but are problematic for guided instruction, as the needs to be addressed are not clear.
- **Random choice** is used when the goal is for students to interact with a range of peers. It is useful when the goal relates to attitudes and opinions. Having said that, random choice has the same drawbacks as student choice—namely that the groups may not have the range of experience and interest required for the task.

How Many Students Should Be in a Guided Instruction Group?

Our rule of thumb is four. Of course, we recognize that classrooms don't divide into groups of four conveniently, especially when groups are formed based on students' instructional needs. There might be one or two groups of five students or one or two groups of three students. We also recognize that at times an individual student may need a level of support that requires a one-to-one experience. This requirement is a challenge if it occurs regularly, as there is an economy of scale that doesn't allow for lots of prolonged individual instruction. When the need is such that a learner requires this level of attention, other systems should kick in, such as the school's response-to-intervention plan (Fisher & Frey, 2010).

We also don't like to have more than five students for most guided instruction tasks. Our experience suggests that when groups get to be six or bigger, the risk of leaving a student out increases. When groups get bigger, more students are excluded from the conversation, mostly due to time constraints. For example, Fay, Garrod, and Carletta (2000) note that when group size was 10, "communication is like monologue and members are influenced most by the dominant speaker" (p. 481). As teachers, that's clearly not what we want. We need to keep group size small enough to ensure that every student benefits from the effect that guided instruction has on their learning.

In addition, a smaller group ensures that we as teachers can consider what questions, prompts, or cues to offer at a moment in time. We have seen "guided instruction" that really was lots of individual instruction at a small table. The teacher was working incredibly hard, but having to scaffold the learning of seven or eight students was too much. It was akin to watching a juggler trying to keep all the balls in the air. This becomes more problematic as students may stop communicating with each other and instead only dialogue with the teacher. The end result is an unsatisfying experience for both students and the teacher, who feel that their goals were not accomplished.

How Long Should Groups Stay Together?

This is a more complex question and depends, to a significant degree, on the types of tasks students complete as part of their guided instruction. Some tasks are one-time events, and students should be regrouped following the completion of the task. Other tasks require much more review and practice, and thus the groups should be together longer.

We tend to keep groups together for about six weeks to receive the kinds of instruction outlined in this book. Of course, we can move individual students from group to group based on need and their individual progress. Remember that we recommend that groups be formed based on formative assessment information. This means that you'll want to regularly collect formative assessment data to determine when and how groups should be created. Of course, these formative assessments are not limited to tests, but include oral language, questioning, writing, and projects or performances (see, for example, Fisher & Frey, 2007).

Is a Student Only Allowed to Be in One Group?

No! Some students need access to multiple guided instruction events to develop their understanding. As teachers, we have to get past the "single dose" phenomenon. Some students don't need guided instruction on a given day based on the topic of investigation; others need a great deal of guided instruction. "Fair" doesn't mean "equal"; fair is getting what you need. For education to be responsive, we must be willing to assign unequal resources for unequal needs. The fact is that students don't exist on the same plane and at a given time may require more (or less) attention in the form of guided instruction. Keep in mind that the purpose of guided instruction is to offer temporary scaffolds that boost students to a higher level of understanding and accomplishment. That means that as responsive educators we need to be willing to provide these scaffolds in a timely and meaningful way. Too much scaffolding is a waste of instructional time; too little will not sufficiently move students to a higher level of understanding. When the unit of analysis is the student, not the time, then different dosage levels become the norm.

Summing Up

Guided instruction builds student confidence and competence; there is no doubt of that. But it is essential to view it within the larger context of how we build students' conceptual knowledge. There are times during the day when we are building background knowledge. At other times we are introducing new information and linking it to prior knowledge by establishing purposes. As part of the classroom experience, students spend time with one another in productive group work where they can clarify and refine what they know. Guided instruction serves as a linchpin across all these experiences. As we build background knowledge, we ask questions to check for understanding. As we establish purpose, we offer cues to direct students' attention to what they should learn. As we introduce new information, we temporarily release some of the cognitive responsibility to see what they understand thus far, and what needs to be further clarified. As students work with one another collaboratively, we position ourselves into these group conversations, offering guided instruction to move the group along in their work. And at times we purposefully create a small group of students who join us in a more intimate instructional arrangement so we can witness their thinking as we dialogue with them, providing scaffolds as needed.

Guided instruction, then, is not something that occurs only during a fixed time of day. It is the bread and butter of what we do as teachers. Much like adults teaching young children how to ride a bike, guided instruction is running alongside, grasping the back of the bike seat to steady it when the riders get wobbly, exhorting them to pedal faster, and then letting go when they regain control. To be sure, it is both an art and a science, and by no means something that we successfully accomplish 100 percent of the time. But a clear understanding of the instructional moves we make and the rationale we use for doing so results over time in learners who can accomplish more than they could the day before.

References

Alfassi, M. (2004). Reading to learn: The effects of combined strategies instruction on high school students. *Journal of Educational Research*, *97*(4), 171–184.

Alvermann, D. E., & Boothby, P. R. (1982, September). *A strategy for making content reading successful: Grades 4–6.* Paper presented at the annual meeting of the Plains Regional Conference of the International Reading Association, Omaha, NE.

Amdahl, K., & Loats, J. (1995). *Algebra unplugged.* Broomfield, CO: Clearwater Publishing.

Anderson, J. R. (1976). *Language, memory, and thought.* Hillsdale, NJ: Erlbaum.

Anderson, L. W., & Krathwohl, D. R. (Eds.). (2001). *A taxonomy for learning, teaching and assessing: A revision of Bloom's taxonomy of educational objectives: Complete edition.* New York: Longman.

Applebee, A. N., & Langer, J. (1983). Instructional scaffolding: Reading and writing as natural language activities. *Language Arts*, *60*(2), 168–175.

Arzarello, F., Paola, D., Robutti, O., & Sabena, C. (2009). Gestures as semiotic resources in the mathematics classroom. *Educational Studies in Mathematics*, *70*(2), 97–109.

Bandura, A. (1965). Influence of models' reinforcement contingencies on the acquisition of imitative responses. *Journal of Personality and Social Psychology*, *1*, 589–595.

Bandura, A. (1977). *Social learning theory.* Englewood Cliffs, NJ: Prentice-Hall.

Barker, M. R., Bailey, J. S., & Lee, N. (2004). The impact of verbal prompts on child safety-belt use in shopping carts. *Journal of Applied Behavioral Analysis*, *37*(4), 527–530.

Batten, J. (2002). *The man who ran faster than everyone: The story of Tom Longboat.* Plattsburgh, NY: Tundra Books.

Benson, B. (1997). Scaffolding. *English Journal, 86*(7), 126–127.

Bereiter, C., & Scardamalia, M. (1992). Cognition and curriculum. In P. Jackson (Ed.), *Handbook of research on curriculum* (pp. 517–542). New York: Macmillan.

Bianchi-Berthouze, N., & Kleinsmith, A. (2003). A categorical approach to affective gesture recognition. *Connection Science, 15*(4), 259–269.

Block, C. C. (2004). *Teaching comprehension: The comprehension process approach.* Boston: Allyn & Bacon.

Block, C., Parris, S. R., & Whiteley, C. S. (2008). CPMs: A kinesthetic comprehension strategy. *The Reading Teacher, 61*(6), 460–470.

Bloom, B. S. (1956). *Taxonomy of educational objectives: The classification of educational goals: Handbook I, cognitive domain.* New York: Longman.

Bomer, R. (1999). Conferring with struggling readers: The test of our craft, courage, and hope. *New Advocate, 12*(1), 21–38.

Bransford, J. D., Brown, A. L., & Cocking, R. R. (Eds.). (1999). *How people learn: Brain, mind, experience, and school.* Committee on Developments in the Science of Learning and Committee on Learning Research and Educational Practice. Washington, DC: National Academy Press.

Brookhart, S. M. (2008). *How to give effective feedback to your students.* Alexandria, VA: ASCD.

Brophy, J. (1987). *On motivating students* [Occasional paper no. 101. East Lansing, MI: Institute for Research on Teaching, Michigan State University. [ERIC Document Number ED 276724]

Brophy, J. (2010). *Motivating students to learn.* New York: Routledge.

Bruer, J. T. (1997). Education and the brain: A bridge too far. *Educational Researcher 26*(8), 4–16.

Burian, P. K. (2004). *Mastering digital photography and imaging.* Hoboken, NJ: Sybex.

Burruss, G., & Hecht, M. (2005, November 15). Evaluation of teaching statistics through visual cues. Paper presented at the annual meeting of the American Society of Criminology, Royal York, Toronto, Canada. Retrieved November 26, 2009, from http://www.allacademic.com/meta/p33451_index.html

Calvo-Merino, B., Glaser, D. E., Grezes, J., Passingham, R. E., & Haggard, P. (2005). Action observation and acquired motor skills: An fMRI study with expert dancers. *Cerebral Cortex, 15*(8), 1243–1249.

Cazden, C. B. (1988). *Classroom discourse: The language of teaching and learning.* Portsmouth, NH: Heinemann.

Chase, W. G., & Simon, H. A. (1973). Perception in chess. *Cognitive Psychology, 4*, 55–81.

Choksy, L. (1999). *The Kodály Method I: Comprehensive music education.* Upper Saddle River, NJ: Prentice-Hall.

Clay, M. M. (2001). *Change over time in children's literacy.* Portsmouth, NH: Heinemann.

Corsini, D. A. (1972). Kindergarten children's use of spatial-positional, verbal, and nonverbal cues for memory. *Journal of Educational Psychology, 63*(4), 353–357.

Coyne, M. D., Zipoli, R. P., Jr., Chard, D. J., Faggella-Luby, M., Ruby, M., Santoro, L. E., et al. (2009). Direct instruction of comprehension: Instructional examples from intervention research on listening and reading comprehension. *Reading & Writing Quarterly, 25*, 221–245.

Davey, B. (1987). Think aloud: Modeling cognitive processes for reading comprehension. *Journal of Reading, 27*, 44–47.

Davis, B. G. (1993). *Tools for teaching.* San Francisco: Jossey-Bass.

DeKoning, B. B., Tabbers, H. K., Rikers, R. M. J. P., & Paas, F. (2009). Towards a framework for attention cueing in instructional animations: Guidelines for research and design. *Educational Psychology Review, 21*(2), 113–140.

Dewitz, P., Jones, J., & Leahy, S. (2009). Comprehension strategy instruction in core reading programs. *Reading Research Quarterly, 44*(2), 102–126.

Dijkstra, K., Kaschak, M. P., & Zwaan, R. A. (2007). Body posture facilitates retrieval of autobiographical memories. *Cognition, 102*(1), 139–149.

Dixon, R. C., Carnine, D., & Kameenui, E. J. (1993). Using scaffolding to teach writing. *Educational Leadership, 51*(3), 100–101.

Duffy, G. G. (2003). *Explaining reading: A resource for teaching concepts, skills, and strategies.* New York: Guilford.

Duffy, G. G., & Roehler, L. R. (1989). Why strategy instruction is so difficult and what we need to do about it. In C. B. McCormick, G. Miller, & M. Pressley (Eds.), *Cognitive strategy research: From basic research to educational applications* (pp. 133–154). New York: Springer-Verlag.

Duke, N. K., & Pearson, P. D. (2002). Effective practices for developing reading comprehension. In A. E. Farstup & S. J. Samuels (Eds.), *What research has to say about reading instruction* (pp. 205–242). Newark, DE: International Reading Association.

Durkin, D. (1978–79). What classroom observations reveal about comprehension instruction. *Reading Research Quarterly, 15*, 481–533.

Elbers, E. (1996). Cooperation and social context in adult-child interaction. *Learning and Instruction, 6*, 281–286.

Eley, M. G., & Norton, P. (2004). The structuring of initial descriptions or demonstrations in the teaching of procedures. *International Journal of Mathematical Education in Science and Technology, 35*(6), 843–866.

Elliott, R., & Dolan, R. J. (1999). Differential neural responses during performance of matching and nonmatching to sample tasks at two delay intervals. *Journal of Neuroscience, 19*, 5066–5073.

Emig, J. (1971). *The composing process of twelfth graders.* NCTE research report no. 13. Urbana, IL: National Council of Teachers of English.

Ericsson, K. A., & Kintsch, W. (1995). Long-term working memory. *Psychological Review, 102*, 211–245.

Fay, N., Garrod, S., & Carletta, J. (2000). Group discussion as interactive dialogue or as social monologue: The influence of group size. *Psychological Science, 11*, 481–486.

Fisher, D., & Frey, N. (2003). Writing instruction for struggling adolescent writers: A gradual release model. *Journal of Adolescent and Adult Literacy, 46,* 396–407.

Fisher, D., & Frey, N. (2007). *Checking for understanding: Formative assessment techniques for your classroom.* Alexandria, VA: ASCD.

Fisher, D., & Frey, N. (2008). *Better learning through structured teaching: A framework for the gradual release of responsibility.* Alexandria, VA: ASCD.

Fisher, D., & Frey, N. (2009a). *Background knowledge: The missing piece of the comprehension puzzle.* Portsmouth, NH: Heinemann.

Fisher, D., & Frey, N. (2009b). Feed up, back, forward. *Educational Leadership, 67*(3), 20–25.

Fisher, D., & Frey, N. (2010). *Enhancing RtI: How to ensure success with classroom instruction and intervention.* Alexandria, VA: ASCD.

Fisher, D., Frey, N., & Anderson, H. (2010). Thinking and comprehending in the mathematics classroom. In K. Ganske & D. Fisher (Eds.), *Comprehension across the curriculum: Perspectives and practices K–12* (pp. 146–159). New York: Guilford.

Fisher, D., Frey, N., & Lapp, D. (2009). *In a reading state of mind: Brain research, teacher modeling, and comprehension instruction.* Newark, DE: International Reading Association.

Fisher, D., Frey, N., & Rothenberg, C. (2008). *Content area conversations: How to plan discussion-based lessons for diverse language learners.* Alexandria, VA: ASCD.

Fisher, D., Frey, N., & Young, L. (2007). *After school content literacy project for California.* Sacramento: California Department of Education.

Flanders, N. (1970). *Analyzing teacher behavior.* Reading, MA: Addison-Wesley.

Flood, J., Lapp, D., Flood, S., & Nagel, G. (1992). Am I allowed to group? Using flexible patterns for effective instruction. *The Reading Teacher, 45,* 608–616.

Frey, N., Fisher, D., & Everlove, S. (2009). *Productive group work: How to engage students, build teamwork, and promote understanding.* Alexandria, VA: ASCD.

Gagne, R. M. (1985). *The conditions of learning and theory of instruction.* New York: CBS College Publishing.

Gallese, V., & Lakoff, G. (2005). The brain's concepts: The role of the sensory–motor system in conceptual knowledge. *Cognitive Neuropsychology, 22,* 455–479.

Gianetto, J. L., & Rule, A. J. (2005). Using object boxes to teach about Middle Eastern antiquity. *Social Studies and the Young Learner, 17*(4), 4–7.

Gladwell, M. (2005). *Blink: The power of thinking without thinking.* New York: Little, Brown.

Graff, G., & Birkenstein, C. (2006). *They say/I say: The moves that matter in academic writing.* New York: W. W. Norton & Company.

Greenfield, P. M. (1999). Historical change and cognitive change: A two-decade follow-up study in Zinacantan, a Maya community in Chiapas, Mexico. *Mind, Culture, and Activity, 6,* 92–98.

Guemez, J., Fiolhais, C., & Fiolhais, M. (2009). Toys in physics lectures and demonstrations: A brief review. *Physics Education, 44*(1), 53–64.

Guthrie, J. T., Wigfield, A., & Barbosa, P. (2004). Increasing reading comprehension and engagement through concept-oriented reading instruction. *Journal of Educational Psychology, 96*(3), 403–423.

Harmon, J. M., Wood, K. D., Hedrick, W. B., Vintinner, J., & Willeford, T. (2009). Interactive word walls: More than just reading the writing on the walls. *Journal of Adolescent & Adult Literacy, 52*(5), 398–408.

Hattie, J., & Timperley, H. (2007). The power of feedback. *Review of Educational Research, 77*, 81–112.

Hebb, D. O. (1949). *The organization of behavior.* New York: Wiley.

Heuser, D. (2000). Reworking the workshop for math and science. *Educational Leadership, 58*(1), 34–37.

Hogan, K., & Pressley, M. (Eds.). (1997). *Scaffolding student learning: Instructional approaches and issues.* Cambridge, MA: Brookline Books.

Hung, D., Chen, V., & Lim, S. H. (2009). Unpacking the hidden efficacies of learning in productive failure. *Learning Inquiry, 3*(1), 1–19.

Hwang, W. Y., Su, J. H., Hwang, Y. M., & Dong, J. J. (2009). A study of multi-representation of geometry problem solving with virtual manipulatives and whiteboard system. *Educational Technology & Society, 12*(3), 229–247.

Iacoboni, M. (2008). *Mirroring people: The new science of how we connect with others.* New York: Farrar, Straus & Giroux.

Jonassen, D. H., Tessmer, M., & Hannum, W. H. (1999). *Task analysis methods for instructional design.* Mahwah, NJ: Lawrence Erlbaum Associates.

Kapur, M. (2008). Productive failure. *Cognition and Instruction, 26*(3), 379–424.

Kelley, C. M., & Jacoby, L. L. (1996). Adult egocentrism: Subjective experience versus analytic bases for judgment. *Journal of Memory and Language, 35*(2), 157–175.

Kirschner, P. A., Sweller, J., & Clark, R. E. (2006). Why minimal guidance during instruction does not work: An analysis of the failure of constructivist, discovery, problem-based, experiential, and inquiry-based teaching. *Educational Psychologist, 41*(2), 75–86.

Kirwan, B., & Ainsworth, L. (Eds.). (1992). *A guide to task analysis.* London: Taylor and Francis.

Knudsen, E. I. (2007). Fundamental components of attention. *Annual Review of Neuroscience, 30*(1), 57–78.

LaBerge, D., & Samuels, S. J. (1974). Toward a theory of automatic information processing in reading. *Cognitive Psychology, 6*(2), 293–323.

Larkin, M. (2002). Using scaffolded instruction to optimize learning. Arlington, VA: ERIC Clearinghouse on Disabilities and Gifted Education. (ERIC Document Reproduction Service No. ED474301)

Lewis, R. (2001). Classroom discipline and student responsibility: The students' view. *Teaching and Teacher Education, 17*, 307–319.

Lipscomb, L., Swanson, J., & West, A. (2004). Scaffolding. In M. Orey (Ed.), *Emerging perspectives on learning, teaching, and technology*. Retrieved November 27, 2009, from http://projects.coe .uga.edu/epltt/

Los Angeles County Office of Education. (2009). TESA website. Available: http://www.lacoe.edu/ orgs/165

Mally, K. K. (2006). Teachers … Get a cue! *Teaching Elementary Physical Education, 17*(4), 38–39.

Maloch, B. (2002). Scaffolding student talk: One teacher's role in literature discussion groups. *Reading Research Quarterly, 37*(1), 94–112.

Manning, M. (2004). Visual cues. *Teaching Pre K–8, 34*(6), 91–92.

Marzano, R. J. (2004). *Building background knowledge for academic achievement: Research on what works in schools.* Alexandria, VA: ASCD.

Medina, J. (2008). *Brain rules: 12 principles for surviving and thriving at work, home and school.* Seattle, WA: Pear Press.

Miller, G. A. (1956). The magical number seven, plus or minus two: Some limits on our capacity for processing information. *Psychological Review, 63*, 81–97.

Nathan, M. J., & Petrosino, A. (2003). Expert blind spot among preservice teachers. *American Educational Research Journal, 40*(4), 905–928.

Naylor, P. R. (1991). *Shiloh.* New York: Dell Books for Young Readers.

Oakes, J. (2005). *Keeping track: How schools structure inequality* (2nd ed.). New Haven, CT: Yale University Press.

Ormond, T. C. (1992). The prompt/feedback package in physical education. *Journal of Physical Education, Recreation & Dance, 63*(1), 64–67.

Palincsar, A. M., & Brown, A. L. (1984). Reciprocal teaching of comprehension-fostering and comprehension-monitoring activities. *Cognition and Instruction, 1*(2), 117–175.

Paris, S. G., Cross, D. R., & Lipson, M. Y. (1984). Informed strategies for learning: A program to improve children's reading awareness and comprehension. *Journal of Educational Psychology, 76*, 1239–1252.

Pearson, P. D., & Gallagher, G. (1983). The gradual release of responsibility model of instruction. *Contemporary Educational Psychology, 8*, 112–123.

Peirce, C. S. (1931/1958). *Collected papers of Charles Sanders Peirce.* C. Hartshorne, P. Weiss, & A. Burks (Eds., vols. I–VIII). Cambridge, MA: Harvard University Press.

Piaget, J. (1952). *The origins of intelligence in children.* New York: W. W. Norton.

Pressley, M., Hogan, K., Wharton-McDonald, R., Mistretta, J., & Ettenberger, S. (1996). The challenges of instructional scaffolding: The challenges of instruction that supports student thinking. *Learning Disabilities Research & Practice, 11*(3), 138–146.

Puntambekar, S., & Hübscher, R. (2005). Tools for scaffolding students in a complex environment: What have we gained and what have we missed? *Educational Psychologist, 40*(1), 1–12.

Ragoff, B. (1990). *Apprenticeship in thinking: Cognitive development in social context.* New York: Oxford University Press.

Rand, A. (2009). *Anthem.* Rockford, IL: BN Publishing.

Raphael, T. E. (1982). Teaching children question-answering strategies. *The Reading Teacher, 36,* 186–191.

Raphael, T. E. (1984). Teaching learners about sources of information for answering questions. *Journal of Reading, 27,* 303–311.

Raphael, T. E. (1986). Teaching children question-answer relationships, revisited. *The Reading Teacher, 39,* 516–522.

Raphael, T. E., & Au, K. H. (2005). QAR: Enhancing comprehension and test taking across grades and content areas. *The Reading Teacher, 59*(3), 206–221.

Read, J. D., & Barnsley, R. H. (1977). Remember Dick & Jane? Memory for elementary school readers. *Canadian Journal of Behavioral Science, 9,* 361–370.

Reynolds, R. E., & Anderson, R. C. (1982). Influence of questions on the allocation of attention during reading. *Journal of Educational Psychology, 74*(5), 623–632.

Rieber, R. W. (Ed.). (1998). *The collected works of L. S. Vygotsky: Volume 5: Child psychology.* New York: Springer.

Robinson, D. H. (1998). Graphic organizers as aids to text learning. *Reading Research and Instruction, 37,* 85–105.

Rodgers, E. (2004/05). Interactions that scaffold reading performance. *Journal of Literacy Research, 36*(4), 501–532.

Roser, N. L., Hoffman, J. V., Labbo, L. D., & Farest, C. (1992). Language charts: A record of story time talk. *Language Arts, 69*(1), 44–52.

Roth, W. M., McRobbie, C. J., Lucas, K. B., & Boutonne, S. (1997). Why may students fail to learn from demonstrations? A social practice perspective on learning in physics. *Journal of Research in Science Teaching, 34*(5), 509–533.

Seligman, M. E. P. (1975). *Helplessness: On depression, development, and death.* San Francisco: W. H. Freeman.

Squire, L. R., & Kandel, E. R. (2000). *Memory: From mind to molecules.* New York: W. H. Freeman.

Standing, L., Conezio, J., & Haber, R. N. (1970). Perception and memory for pictures: Single-trial learning of 2,500 visual stimuli. *Psychonomic Science, 19,* 73–74.

Stenberg, G. (2006). Conceptual and perceptual factors in the picture superiority effect. *European Journal of Cognitive Psychology, 18,* 813–847.

Sweller, J. (2003). Evolution of human cognitive architecture. In B. Ross (Ed.), *The psychology of learning and motivation* (Vol. 43, pp. 215–266). San Diego, CA: Academic.

Tan, N. J. (1994). Analysis of elementary geometry teaching materials. Paper presented at the New Elementary Mathematics Curriculum in Taiwan.

Tate, M. L. (2003). *Worksheets don't grow dendrites*. Thousand Oaks, CA: Corwin Press.

Thompson, I. (2009). Scaffolding in the writing center: A microanalysis of an experienced tutor's verbal and nonverbal tutoring strategies. *Written Communication, 26*(4), 417–453.

Tomlinson, C. A., & McTighe, J. (2006). *Integrating differentiated instruction and Understanding by Design: Connecting content and kids*. Alexandria, VA: ASCD.

Vygotsky, L. S. (1962). *Thought and language*. Cambridge, MA: MIT Press.

Vygotsky, L. S. (1978). *Mind in society*. (M. Cole, Trans.). Cambridge, MA: Harvard University Press.

Walsh, J. A., & Sattes, B. D. (2005). *Quality questioning: Research-based practice to engage every learner*. Thousand Oaks, CA: Corwin Press.

Wansink, B., & Sobal, J. (2007). Mindless eating: The 200 daily food decisions we overlook. *Environment and Behavior, 39*(1), 106–123.

Watkins, C. L., & Slocum, T. A. (2003). The components of direct instruction. *Journal of Direct Instruction, 3*(2), 75–110.

Weismer, S. E., & Kesketh, L. J. (1993). The influence of prosodic and gestural cues on novel word acquisition by children with specific language impairment. *Journal of Speech and Hearing Research, 36*(5), 1013–1025.

Wellcome Trust. (n.d.). The dancers brain [Online article]. Available: http://www.youramazingbrain.org/Brainbody/dancers.htm

Wiesel, E. (2006). *Night* (Rev. ed.). New York: Hill and Wang.

Wilhelm, J. (2001). *Improving comprehension with think-aloud strategies*. New York: Scholastic.

Williams, K. C. (2009). *Elementary classroom management: A student-centered approach to leading and learning*. Thousand Oaks, CA: Sage.

Willingham, D. (2008). When and how neuroscience applies to education. *Phi Delta Kappan, 89*, 421–423.

Wood, D., Bruner, J. S., & Ross, G. (1976). The role of tutoring and problem solving. *Journal of Child Psychology and Psychiatry, 17*, 89–100.

Wood, D., & Wood, H. (1996). Vygotsky, tutoring and learning. *Oxford Review of Education, 22*(1), 5–16.

Yeh, S. S. (2006). High-stakes testing: Can rapid assessment reduce the pressure? *Teachers College Record, 108*, 621–661.

Zhao, R., & Orey, M. (1999). The scaffolding process: Concepts, features, and empirical studies. Unpublished manuscript, University of Georgia.

Zimmerman, B. (2008). Investigating self-regulation and motivation: Historical background, methodological developments, and future prospects. *American Educational Research Journal, 45*(1), 166–183.

Index

Information in figures is indicated by *f*.

About the Authors

Douglas Fisher

Douglas Fisher, PhD, is a professor of language and literacy education in the Department of Teacher Education at San Diego State University and a classroom teacher at Health Sciences High & Middle College. He is a member of the California Reading Hall of Fame and is the recipient of a Celebrate Literacy Award from the International Reading Association, the Farmer Award for Excellence in Writing from the National Council of Teachers of English, and a Christa McAuliffe Award for Excellence in Teacher Education from the American Association of State Colleges and Universities. He has published numerous articles on improving student achievement, and his books include *Creating Literacy-Rich Schools for Adolescents* (with Gay Ivey), *Checking for Understanding* (with Nancy Frey), and *Content-Area Conversations* (with Carol Rothenberg and Nancy Frey). He can be reached at dfisher@mail.sdsu.edu.

Nancy Frey

Nancy Frey, PhD, is a professor of literacy in the School of Teacher Education at San Diego State University and a classroom teacher at Health Sciences High & Middle College. Before joining the university faculty, Nancy was a special education teacher in the Broward County (Florida) Public Schools, where she taught students at the elementary and middle school levels. She later worked for the Florida Department of Education on a statewide project for supporting students with disabilities in a general education curriculum. Nancy is a recipient of the Christa McAuliffe Award for Excellence in Teacher Education from the American Association of State Colleges and Universities and the Early Career Award from the National Reading Conference. Her research interests include reading and literacy, assessment, intervention, and curriculum design. She has published many articles and books on literacy and instruction, including *Productive Group Work* and *Better Learning Through Structured Teaching* (both with Doug Fisher). She can be reached at nfrey@mail.sdsu.edu.

Related ASCD Resources: Guided Instruction

At the time of publication, the following ASCD resources were available; for the most up-to-date information about ASCD resources, go to www.ascd.org. ASCD stock numbers are noted in parentheses.

Print Products

Advancing Formative Assessment in Every Classroom: A Guide for Instructional Leaders by Connie M. Moss and Susan M. Brookhart (#109031)

Better Learning Through Structured Teaching: A Framework for the Gradual Release of Responsibility by Douglas Fisher and Nancy Frey (#108010)

Checking for Understanding: Formative Assessment Techniques for Your Classroom by Douglas Fisher and Nancy Frey (#107023)

Educational Leadership, December 2007/January 2008, Informative Assessment (#108023)

How to Give Effective Feedback to Your Students by Susan M. Brookhart (#108019)

What Teachers Really Need to Know About Formative Assessment by Laura Greenstein (#110017)

Videos and DVDs

Assessment for 21st Century Learning DVD Set (three 30-minute DVDs, each with a professional development program) (#610010S25)

Balanced Assessment: Improving Student Achievement and Standardized Test Results Bundle (three-tape video set; one DVD; one print Facilitator's Guide and one online Facilitator's Guide) (#704451)

The Whole Child Initiative helps schools and communities create learning environments that allow students to be healthy, safe, engaged, supported, and challenged. To learn more about other books and resources that relate to the whole child, visit www.wholechildeducation.org.

For additional resources, visit us on the World Wide Web (http://www.ascd .org), send an e-mail message to member@ascd.org, call the ASCD Service Center (1-800-933-ASCD or 703-578-9600, then press 2), send a fax to 703-575-5400, or write to Information Services, ASCD, 1703 N. Beauregard St., Alexandria, VA 22311-1714 USA.